HELP! I'M A TEENAGER

Self-Esteem For Teens, Stop Teenage Angst, Love Yourself Deeply, Boost Self-Confidence. No More Social Anxiety For Teens

REBECCA COLLINS

CONTENTS

Disclaimer	v
Author Profile	vii
Introduction	ix
1. Love Yourself Deeply - Why You Really Matter	1
2. Teenage Angst - How To Stop The Downward Spiral And Come Out Winning	11
3. Give Yourself A Break - Letting Go Of Self-Judgment	25
4. Self-Esteem & Self-Confidence - Teenage Superpowers In The Making	36
5. The Most Important Decisions You'll Ever Make	49
6. Body-Shaming, Don't Fall For It	61
7. Bullying Isn't Cool - Stand Up To Intimidation, Repel Ghosting And Defeat The Cancel Culture	72
8. Social Anxiety - Signs, Symptoms, and Solutions	85
9. Help! I'm A Teenager - Powering Up Your Positive	98
Conclusion	111
A Free Gift From Rebecca	115

DISCLAIMER

Although the author and publisher have made every effort to ensure that the information in this book was correct at the time of going to press, the author and publisher do not assume and hereby disclaim any liability to any party for any loss, damage, or disruption caused by errors or omissions, whether such errors or omissions result from negligence, accident, or any other cause.

This publication is meant as a source of valuable information for the reader, however it is not meant as a substitute for direct expert assistance or professional help. If such level of assistance is required, the services of a competent professional should be sought.

Copyright Notice

All rights reserved.

No part of this book may be reproduced in any form or by any electronic or mechanical means, including information storage and retrieval systems, without written permission from the author, except for the use of brief quotations in a book review.

Enjoy the book.

Worldwide Copyright held at Copyright House, London EC2R 8AY, England & The US Copyright Office at Copyright.gov.

Copyright Rebecca Collins 2022 - All rights reserved.

AUTHOR PROFILE

Rebecca Collins is the mother of two teenagers, a boy and a girl. She is also a highly respected personal development coach. Being the only girl in a family of four brothers, she quickly learned to be tough if she wanted to keep up with the boys.

This go-get-it attitude drove her to set up her own company at the age of 25, after completing a degree in business management. She went on to invest in female start-ups and organized online workshops aimed at enabling women to realize their full potential in both their professional and personal lives.

After several years of coaching, geared towards raising self-esteem and self-confidence, Rebecca is an influential voice in the female empowerment niche. She currently resides in Oxford, England.

- Receive Rebecca's Newsletter, FREE "Reclaim Your Power" https://rebecca.subscribemenow.com/

INTRODUCTION

"Teenagers are the most misunderstood people on the planet. They are treated like children and expected to behave like adults."
–Anonymous

You might not know it, but being a teenager is supposed to be fun. It's the time when you get to find your identity, gain your independence, and spread your wings. Does that not sound right in your case?

Are you going through your teenage years like a category 5 hurricane? Does everything feel like it's a mess: friends, dating, school, family life, sports teams, your face? It can be tough when you reach adolescence, and I'm not going to lie about that. From the age of 12 or 13 onward, it's as if you enter into a confusing world where every little thing is hard to deal with and you might even feel miserable a lot of the time.

Being a teenager is like becoming a mutant, as your body and brain suddenly go into overdrive. A potent mix of chemicals start rampaging throughout your system, causing some very weird changes in some very private places. And, as if that's not enough, you also start to get confusing messages from people around you.

Your parents seem to turn into prison wardens, laying down totally unreasonable rules. Friends might also blow hot and cold from one day to the next. And don't even mention dating, which is a total nightmare! I bet you have the feeling that no one out there understands you.

Many people of your age are trying to work through the same kind of issues and don't always get the help or support they need. The bottom line is, no matter what you are facing, you need to help yourself. The way to do this is by nurturing what we call self-love.

You might not know it yet, but most of the problems you are experiencing can be handled a lot better if you take more care of yourself. Self-love is all about appreciating who you are. The way to do this is through your thoughts and actions. Taking care of your health & physical fitness, your emotional wellbeing, and your mental health, are all important steps to creating a stronger sense of self-love.

When you work on each of these aspects, you will see yourself differently, and feel a lot happier. On top of that, you will know when to take care of your own needs and when to avoid sacrificing them to please others. You deserve the best and owe it to yourself to experience that, no matter what kind of influences, temptations, and challenges are heading your way.

Self-love includes two important concepts — self-esteem and self-worth.

When you have high self-esteem, it's easier to feel good about yourself and know your capabilities. You aren't easily talked into doing things you don't agree with or neglect your best interests. Self-worth puts you in the mindset of knowing your true value as a person and being able to avoid situations that undermine you or lead you into trouble.

In this book, you'll find a lot of strategies for developing a strong sense of self-love and greater confidence in your own potential. As you go through the chrysalis phase of your teenage years, you probably have so many doubts about the choices you need to make and how you should handle what's going on around you. Don't worry, you'll find a lot of good advice and suggestions here.

You have a lot to contend with and it can all get so overwhelming sometimes. I wonder how many of the following issues you are struggling with or have experienced:

- Anxiety/Stress
- Depression
- Bullying (at school or online)
- Your sexual identity
- Peer pressure
- Alcohol or drug consumption
- Body image issues
- Academic problems
- Parental pressure
- Trust issues
- Lack of motivation
- Dealing with failure
- Low self-esteem
- Low energy levels

Everything I've just mentioned are common problems teenagers can face all over the world and knowing how to handle them isn't easy at all. But the one thing that is guaranteed to help you to navigate these is a stronger sense of self-love.

You can, and should, be enjoying your life, even though you might not think that is possible at the moment. I know how hard it is when you feel that way, which is why I'm going to be sharing a lot of useful strategies here with you.

We are going to take a look at why you really **DO** matter, and how you can make a difference in this world. Next, we'll tackle feelings of **anxiety** and the constant need you might have to **compare yourself** to others. I'll help you to re-focus on the most important person in life - **YOU**!

I'll be teaching you some hacks on how to put things into little boxes, instead of letting everything pile up on top of you like one big mountain of **stress and chaos**. You can also pick up some empowering tips on how to stop being so hard on yourself - that's the last thing you need right now.

You will find a lot of useful information about how to improve your **self-confidence,** even if you don't always believe it, and find ways to build up your self-esteem. When it comes to making sound decisions, you'll discover the best way to make **the right choices** for you, not for anyone else.

I'm going to be looking at the serious issues of **body shaming** and **bullying**, which I'm sure many of you have suffered from, and help you to find ways to get over these painful experiences.

And, finally, we will take a look at the benefits of **positive thinking** and developing a **healthy mindset.**

All you need to do is remember that your teenage years won't last forever. Before you know it, you will be a fully-fledged, independent adult. Until then, why not pick up some of the important life skills that will help you to charter these turbulent teenage years and come out smiling!

Life is supposed to be fun, and don't you forget it!

Free for you.

10 Weekly Issues of Rebecca's life-changing newsletter "Reclaim Your Power" Rebecca covers Self Love, Self Esteem, Making Friends, Getting Your Life Back & Living A Life of Freedom.

https://rebecca.subscribemenow.com/

Scan Me..

1

LOVE YOURSELF DEEPLY - WHY YOU REALLY MATTER

*"I am somebody. I am me. I like being me.
And I need nobody to make me somebody."*
– Louis L'Amour

A lot of top celebrities had a really rough time growing up. Some were extremely poor, lived in trailer parks, had absent parents, or dropped out of school. As teenagers, none of them felt like they were somebody and found life very hard.

Celebs like Leonardo DiCaprio, Nicki Minaj, Hilary Swank, and Mark Wahlberg often talk about the problems they had to deal with as teenagers and how they managed to find success, despite that.

Not everyone has it easy from early on, and the teen years can be extremely challenging for you as a person. Apart from things like coming from a dysfunctional family, economic problems, or social inequalities, you also have to deal with that rocky transition from childhood to adulthood. It can bring you face-to-face with your insecurities as you try to fit into a world that can often seem very demanding. It's during these years that you need to discover who you are and to build on that. If you don't like the person you think you are, this can cause a lot of problems for years to come.

When I was around 14 years old, I had no idea how to love myself. I was a skinny, spotty, tomboy with hardly any confidence. I remember looking in the mirror and not liking what I saw at all. I certainly wasn't the most popular girl in the class and kept myself to myself most of the time. Boys weren't interested in me and I felt a kind of self-loathing. I used to think, "If only I was prettier, taller, more bubbly... everything would be so much better."

I really wanted to be liked by my friends so I did a couple of things I'm not proud of, like skipping off school once or twice and stealing chocolate bars from the local sweet shop. Harmless antics, you might say, but looking back, I can see that it was all about trying to fit in. Luckily, I was pretty smart academically so did well at school, but no one seemed to care at home. My parents were more concerned about the mess in my bedroom than the state of my emotional wellbeing, or that's how I felt at the time.

Your story

Your story will be different from mine, but I'm sure you are still going through situations that are seriously getting you down. You don't feel comfortable in your own skin, aren't sure how to behave around others, don't understand your emotions, and are loaded down by a lot of pressure and stress in your life. You have to get the grades, do the chores, win the game, be liked, behave: all of this when you're struggling just to get up in the morning

No one tells you that you have to love yourself if you want to get through life. Growing up as a kid, you have people around you giving you all the love you need (hopefully). You don't have that strong awareness of the self because you are still developing and maturing. By the time you hit your teens, it's like you are dumped on some desert island and just expected to 'get on with it'.

How are you supposed to start respecting, loving, and honoring yourself when you haven't had to do it before? How do you navigate the ups and downs of everything you are facing if you don't have any sense of identity and self-worth? What if you just don't like yourself?

Teenage years are a transitional phase and that's why they are difficult to get through, but it can be done. No matter what situation you are in, if you can build a strong appreciation of who you are, this will guide you through all of the challenges. It's a learning process and you are going to make mistakes, but that's what life is all about.

Self-love doesn't mean being arrogant or selfish. It's nothing to do with feeling good because you got a new iPhone or the latest brand of jogging pants.

That's all cool, but these are momentary niceties that don't change how you feel deep within yourself. Self-love is more of a solid base that you build when you do anything that supports your physical, psychological, and emotional growth.

When you act with self-love as a priority, you can avoid negative thoughts and feelings, stop yourself from developing bad habits, and feel more centered. You learn to accept and love who you are while trying to improve daily. If you can form this strong base, you will feel happier within yourself and enjoy life a whole lot more.

You have value as a human being and are worthy of love and respect, so learn how to start loving yourself with the tips I'm going to share below.

Stop criticizing yourself

You'll find plenty of critics out there who can do that for you! When you constantly obsess over your flaws, you are making them more important than they really are. If you keep telling yourself that your ears are too big, or you aren't tall enough, it's not surprising that you feel dissatisfied.

The truth is that your body is part of who you are and you should be proud of it. The same goes for your abilities – reminding yourself every day of your weaknesses feeds into this negative cycle and will make you feel worse about yourself overall.

It only causes you pain when you self-criticize and you aren't cultivating a positive mindset. To do that, you need to stop listening to the negative voice inside you – the one that tells you how you are too slow, too fat, too ugly, or too dumb. Press that mute button when these thoughts start to invade your mind and turn your thinking around by focusing on your good points. Give yourself the thumbs up for your sporting talents, your willingness to help others, or your great drawing skills, and silence that inner critic. You don't need it.

Learn to forgive yourself

You are going to make quite a few mistakes during your passage from childhood to adulthood and it's all part of the learning game so don't be too hard on yourself. We all slip up or make bad choices now and again and you are no exception. Instead of lingering over your bad grades, the lie you told, the friend you let down, ease up a bit. As long as you are trying your best and understand what you did wrong and how to make it better, there is no need to beat yourself up.

Whatever has happened, you have to learn to forgive yourself. This means saying:

I messed up but that doesn't make me a bad person.

I know what mistake I made and can learn from that.

I'm not perfect and forgive myself for what I did/didn't do.

As you go through this time of your life, you'll learn a lot of lessons, and one of the most important is self-forgiveness. When you can accept your wrongdoings, you can grow from them and move on.

Practice self-care

You need to take care of yourself if you want to feel good. If you've ever owned a pet, you'll know that they need some basic things in life to survive, like food, water, shelter, and a lot of love. You also need to take care of your basic needs but no one is going to do it for you. It's up to you to eat nutritious food, sleep enough hours, do regular exercise, and have healthy social connections. When you care for yourself, you are practicing self-love, and that's the most important love of all.

- Start by watching what you eat. Reduce the amount of fast food you consume, which you know isn't good for you, and choose healthier alternatives.
- Work out daily, even if it's just thirty minutes in your bedroom doing some crunches or sit-ups.
- Try to go to sleep a little earlier each night or set yourself a deadline and say, "I'm turning off the lights at 11 pm."
- Choose to stick around people who make you feel good about yourself and not the ones who bring you down.
- What else can you think of doing that would show self-care?

Set your boundaries

In our desire to be liked, we all do things to please others and this can sometimes get us into trouble. That's why it's good to think about what your boundaries are and to keep within them. You have to be strong here and resist the temptation to step over your limits, which is a kind of self-betrayal. When your friends ask you to take part in vandalizing property, take drugs, bully a schoolmate, or lie for them, stop and think about how damaging any of this can be to you and others.

Self-love grows when you draw a line between what you will and won't do, and stay close to your values. It also means stopping others from crossing the line with you and invading your space. Boundaries keep us safe and are a powerful way to show others that we have total respect for ourselves and aren't going to go along with them just to be liked.

Choose your friends

There's going to come a point when you realize that you don't like some of the people you thought were your friends. You might know them from your neighborhood, school, college, or sports team and hang around with them because it's convenient. The thing is, you have a choice about who plays a part in your life and who doesn't. You shouldn't have to put up with a 'frenemy' who isn't good to you, is mean, selfish, or a bad influence.

You can say, "I don't want this person in my life." Once you make the decision, avoid causing a big argument or trolling them on social media. Just gradually distance yourself from them a bit at a time until you feel happy with the amount of space they take up in your life. In time, they will find another friend to annoy. It's extremely important to protect yourself from negative people if you want to build up your self-esteem and practice self-love so don't wait around - do it today!

Reduce your fears

Anything unknown can spike fear, anxiety, and panic. Starting a new school, going on a first date, or taking an important exam are all terrifying prospects that can torture us beforehand. But why worry about things you have no control over? You don't know what the new school will be like - it could be super cool. Your date may or may not go well - only 50% of that is up to you. As for exams, if you have prepared enough and done your best, your best is all you can do.

Things are never usually as bad as you think they are going to be so worrying about them takes all the pleasure away from you. Try being kinder to yourself by thinking about all of the good things that can come out of your next 'unknown' and keep the positivity flowing through your mindset. It's a lot better for your overall well-being to create a mental picture of what will go right instead of what can go wrong. Try it and see!

Give yourself a boost

Why wait for others to praise you, when you can do it yourself? Write down a list of ten things you are proud of or that you like about yourself. It could be anything from having a cute nose to being good at swimming. Maybe you have great cooking skills or are clever at making things with your hands. Perhaps you know a lot about flowers or are a pro at League Of Legends. It doesn't matter what your particular plus points are - just praise yourself as much as you can and be proud. You are special and no one can take that away from you!

Seek Support

Learning to stand on your own two feet is hard so it's a good idea to have someone you can talk to when you feel down or overwhelmed. That could be a parent, another relative, teacher, sports coach, friends, or anyone else you trust. Asking for help and support isn't a sign of weakness - it's a gutsy thing to do. It shows you have the courage to admit when you aren't doing so well and, hopefully, you'll get the help that you need. You don't have to go it alone and people can offer valuable support during your teenage years.

Accept your flaws

Accepting who you are isn't always easy. It means looking at yourself without the rose-tinted glasses and seeing the real you. There is no perfection in life and you don't have to expect that for yourself. When you accept that you aren't good at sports, math, making friends, or playing the guitar, it's an act of self-love. You see, we can only be content with ourselves when we accept the whole package because every little bit makes us who we are. So, embrace those imperfections instead of hating them - they shape and form the uniquely beautiful person that is you.

Become your best friend

Good friends are people we can completely trust and confide in. You might find that no one fits that description in your life at the moment, or you are going through a funny phase where you find it hard to trust others. That's fine because you can become your own best friend by keeping a journal.

I used to keep a diary when I was a teen, where I would write down all of my thoughts and feelings. It felt like a trusted companion to me when I had no one else to talk to. Nowadays, people use daily journals, where they jot down whatever is on their minds. You can buy a journal with activities and prompts designed to improve your wellbeing or even use a blank notebook.

In it, note any negative thoughts and difficult emotions. When you have written them down, spend some time reading them to learn more about who you are. Ask yourself how you can change any negatives to positives and you will be surprised at how easily ideas come into your head.

Love talk

It might sound stupid, but talking to yourself in the mirror is a fantastic way to boost your confidence and nurture self-love. All you have to do is stand in front of the mirror once a day and look straight into your eyes. Now, begin telling yourself how much love you have for the person you see, and how special they are. Learning to love yourself can take time, but this is a very caring way of doing it and you will soon feel better about yourself if you practice it often. You can also talk to your parents through the mirror, or your friends, and express what's on your mind.

Tell your parents you love them and that you forgive them for not always understanding you. Tell your friends how much you love them and apologize for not always being there for them. This might sound a bit weird, but it's allowing you to say things you might find difficult to express face-to-face. When you manage to do it, you feel more content and at peace with the world.

Love life

Just because you are going through a difficult period, it doesn't mean you have to forget about all the joy in life. Stop focusing on your problems for a change and have more fun - life isn't supposed to be miserable.

Organize some time with friends, doing things you all love. Go ice-skating or skateboarding, watch a movie, go see a game, chill out at your favorite snack bar or fast-food restaurant, and remember to laugh. When you have a good time, you feel better about yourself and get a big serotonin kick, which is a natural high!

You DO matter, whether you believe it or not. You are a unique being, full of amazing potential and abilities. It may not seem that way now, but you must hold on to that thought. All of the issues you are facing today: body image, school performance, pressure from parents and friends, desires and needs - all of these are temporary. Life is ever-changing and never dull but one thing always remains constant - your worthiness and value.

It might take you a long time to love yourself deeply and everyone has to go at their own pace. What you need to remember is that you will never be someone else - you will always be you - so learn to love that person from the bottom of your heart and let time do the rest!

Helpful tips

- *Self-love is the most important love in your life.*
- *You deserve to be valued and loved for who you are.*
- *Self-criticism is your worst enemy.*
- *Practicing self-care is an essential part of being happy.*
- *Maintain your boundaries and don't let others invade them.*
- *Forgive your mistakes and learn to move on after failure.*
- *Talk to someone you trust, including yourself.*
- *Enjoy life as much as you can with positive people.*

2

TEENAGE ANGST - HOW TO STOP THE DOWNWARD SPIRAL AND COME OUT WINNING

"Anxiety is the dizziness of freedom."
—Soren Kierkegaard

Life can be stressful for everyone, regardless of age or background. I'm sure you can relate to that feeling of breaking out in a cold sweat, your mind going blank, your palms becoming clammy, and feeling like you want to escape.

This is a perfectly normal physical reaction wired into your brain when it senses that you are in danger. That fight, flight, or freeze mode kicks in automatically, but you soon return to normal when the object of the stress is taken away. It is a common occurrence for many people.

Teenage angst is a bit different from that because you can experience overwhelming feelings of stress and anxiety for no obvious reasons. You might feel that no one understands you and that you are totally alone in the world, which isn't true. Most people your age are going through exactly the same lows but you might not know that because it's not easy for everyone to talk about.

You are at the age where you are trying to figure everything out - who you are, why you are here, and other big questions about the meaning of life. That's a lot to think about and would make anyone anxious. At the same time, you probably have people telling you what to do, like parents, teachers, coaches, and society in general.

This definitely puts pressure on you as you push for independence and still feel held back by rules and regulations. Emotions can get all bottled up inside of you until they explode in mood swings and sudden outbursts.

As a teen, you might be confrontational and disruptive within your family or at school. Parents don't always know how to cope with that and often send confusing messages or butt heads with you in ugly clashes. One minute, your folks are telling you to,"Grow up," and the next, that you are too young to stay out late or borrow the car. It's enough to make anyone want to scream!

All of these worries about your appearance, your identity, and your place in the world can create massive internal stress and even lead to a kind of depression.

It doesn't help that your hormones are currently on overload and causing emotional meltdowns. By the time you reach adulthood, all of this will have settled down and you'll be able to manage stress much easier. But, until then, you need some help to get through it.

The anxiety you feel is very real, and there's no denying that. It can be scary and intense, showing itself in several ways. If you are currently experiencing any of the following, then you will know what I mean:

- Mood swings
- Emotional outbursts
- Being bad-tempered
- Sleeping more than usual
- Loss of appetite
- Feeling self-conscious
- Aches and pains (headaches, stomachaches, etc.,)
- Yelling and ranting
- Being rude or reckless
- Fixating on social media
- Obsessing over your appearance
- Recurring fears and worries
- Trouble concentrating
- Avoiding difficult or new situations
- Drop in grades at school
- Substance abuse

A lot is going on with you that is causing all of the above and you need to understand that. The main culprit is the biological changes you are experiencing as your brain and body try to sync. These adjustments are a necessary part of growing up but along with them comes increased anxiety that can be triggered by everyday situations.

What's going on?

From the ages of 13 to 18, you are still growing and your brain is in the driving seat. The front part, known as the prefrontal cortex, is one of the last areas in your brain to mature. This is the command center for skills like planning, prioritizing, and controlling impulses.

That explains why you find it difficult to do any of the above until you reach the end of adolescence. With all of the chemical, emotional, and social changes you are going through, it's easy to understand why you feel anxious and stressed out.

The truth is that you just don't have the coping mechanisms yet to handle stress in the same way that adults do, which is why you are more prone to emotional highs and lows.

On top of your emotional state, you are also trying to come to terms with physical changes going on in your body. Now, you have to deal with facial hair, acne, and other transformations related to your gender. Boys begin to see their testicles and penises grow in size, they start having wet dreams, and their voices break. Girls start growing breasts and begin to have menstrual periods, as well as seeing hair growth in their pelvic region. It is a very challenging period of your life and no wonder that you feel unsure about everything that is happening to you.

If you want to learn more about all of the physical changes you are likely to be experiencing, you can check out my book **Positive Life Skills For Teens | The Fun Book For Learning Essential Life Skills That Every Teenager Needs To Know.**

What's your situation?

Depending on your situation, you might suffer from more stress than your friends or less. We are all influenced by our surroundings so it's natural to be overcome with anxiety if you are experiencing problems like family circumstances or hardship. Your peer culture can also affect you to a large extent, often pressuring you into doing things you don't want to do or to be someone you aren't.

- Are you a high-flier?

You might have been brought up to be a high achiever and are now struggling with school, your homework, any extracurricular activities, and your overall performance. Many kids are raised with a lot of expectations from their parents to succeed and that pressure can really come to a head during your teenage years.

- Are you anti-everything?

Your struggle for independence may cause you to adopt certain opinions that go against the establishment. As you become more socially aware, the rebel within can awaken and lead you into conflict with people around you. This is all part of the growing phase but adults tend to forget that, and simply expect you to conform to their rules and belief systems.

- Are you being coerced?

As you begin to gain more awareness of your sexuality, you might find yourself curious about sex or even start exploring romantic relationships.

You could also feel you are being coerced or pressured into doing certain activities that you aren't comfortable with and haven't yet found the voice to say no. This is a lot to take on and it can send you spiraling into intense feelings of angst, doubt, and insecurity.

What are you dealing with?

School sucks

Is school becoming a living hell for you?

Are you being bullied, worrying that you don't fit in, being singled out by a teacher, or struggling to keep up in class? Most teens go through a phase where they 'hate' school, for one reason or another. It's where you spend most of your day so even if one little thing is bothering you, it can make your life a misery.

- **Substance abuse**

Do you feel tempted to try recreational drugs?

Some teenagers turn to drugs like marijuana when they feel anxious as a way of coping. It might work in the short term because it numbs the stress they feel but in the long term, it leads to dependence and doesn't solve any problems. It may be legal in some parts of the world to smoke marijuana, but that doesn't make it a healthy way to manage anxiety, no matter what your friends say.

- **Anxiety and depression**

What kind of angst is stopping you from enjoying your life?

It's common for teenagers to feel depressed and have angst at the same time, although these are two different things. You might feel anxious about certain elements of your life and when they are resolved, you feel great. On the other hand, if you still feel depressed without any obvious reason, you might need professional help. It isn't easy to get to the bottom of what is really bothering you so it's always a good idea to talk it through with someone.

- **The scary world**

What recent events have left you feeling afraid?

The world can seem like a scary place and what we see on the news doesn't help. It's frightening when you learn about school shootings, terrorist attacks, and other extreme forms of violence. Anyone would feel unsafe in public if they thought about these things too much and, as a teenager, they are certain to make you feel even less secure in the world. It's good to understand that the world is, in general, a safe place to live in and that such events are very rare if you put them into perspective.

- **Social media**

Do you use too much social media?

A lot of experts blame social media for the increase in anxiety experienced by teens. It might be because you are spending a lot of time comparing yourself to others too much, which eats away at your self-confidence. There's also a lot of unfriendly chat out there and if you get caught up in that, it can be very hurtful. The more time you spend scrolling through your Insta feed and looking at fabulous images of 'perfect' people, the more stress could be building up inside you.

- **Anxiety disorders**

Do you live in a constant state of anxiety?

If so, this can lead to serious mental health problems such as depression, and even suicidal thoughts, which can lead to tragic outcomes so you should treat it very seriously if you feel this is you. You might have frequent panic attacks, are unable to focus at school, suffer from chronic pain or digestive problems, and intense social anxiety. Anybody can be affected by anxiety disorders, regardless of their background, family history, and education.

If you believe that you are suffering from a chronic anxiety disorder, please reach out to a trusted family member or health professional who can give you the right treatment. That might include something called cognitive-behavioral therapy (CBT) and/or a range of

medications. Take your mental health seriously, because it is serious!

How can positive thinking help?

You might believe that positive thinking is some kind of hippy woo woo that doesn't relate to you and your problems. Maybe that's because you haven't taken the time to learn more about its benefits. If so, how do you know if it works or not?

If you want to enjoy your teen years, having a positive outlook can make all the difference, but it's not as simple as thinking happy thoughts. You need to change the bad habits you have gotten into recently: those negative vibes that bring you down

Positive thinking is all about finding a good way to look at your circumstances, no matter what they may be. If you've ever seen the film Forrest Gump with Tom Hanks, you'll recall that the story revolves around someone who always sees the world in a positive light, despite his limitations. These kinds of feel-good movies tell us that life is what we make it, even as a teenager!

As well as helping you to feel better about everything, positive thinking can also improve your memory, help you to make better decisions, and solve problems. Are you ready to give it a try?

I know that you may have a tendency to compare yourself to others and think you aren't good enough. Your self-esteem is probably rock-bottom and you feel hopeless. On top of that, you might find it difficult to control your emotions and even blame your problems on others, lashing out without thinking first. Life will get a lot easier if you start to change your way of thinking.

Me, myself & I

There's only one of you in this world — you are incredibly unique and don't need to compare yourself with anyone else. If you can embrace this idea, it will definitely help you to create a healthy mental attitude. You can start by writing down all of your strengths, whatever they are. Your list could go something like this:

1. I'm good at basketball
2. I have great teeth
3. I make a mean macaroni cheese
4. I'm a fast learner
5. I understand coding

Not everyone has your talents or shares your great attributes and you shouldn't forget that! The temptation to compare yourself with others is OK, as long as they are a good role model for you. But if the person you admire is making you feel inferior, that's not healthy. Instead, set your own standards and be your own influencer because it's your life and you have to live it.

Set SMART goals

You can set yourself doable short-term and long-term goals that will help you to focus on something positive in the future. Let's say you are good at basketball. Why not set a short-term goal of practicing more each week, and a long-term goal of getting onto the school or county team?

It's always good to work towards something that YOU want to do personally as you'll have more drive and motivation to achieve it. You can visualize whatever goal comes to mind and imagine yourself succeeding. Think about that feeling of satisfaction you will have when you get that spot in the team, pass that exam, or can afford that new laptop you have been saving up for.

A tried and tested way of doing this is by setting yourself **SMART** goals. This is an acronym and stands for **Specific, Measurable, Achievable, Realistic,** and **Timely**. Whatever it is you want to accomplish, you can use the SMART goal strategy to get you there. Here's how it works:

- **Specific** - write down exactly what goal you want to achieve
- **Measurable** - think of how you can you measure your progress
- **Achievable** - set a goal you know you can achieve
- **Realistic** - consider how feasible it is
- **Timely** - set yourself reasonable deadlines

The more you work towards achieving your goal, the more confident you will become. Life won't seem half as bad and, in fact, you might even start enjoying it!

Think positive thoughts

When you allow negativity to creep in, it is guaranteed to bring you down. Instead, do yourself a favor and get rid of that mindset and work on creating a positive one. You can turn negatives into positives if you listen to what you are telling yourself and reject whatever is harming your sense of happiness.

Here are some tips to help you do just that:

1 Stop exaggerating the bad things in any situation and focus on the good.

For example, when you get a B instead of the A you wanted in a test, don't tell yourself you are a failure but be happy to have received a decent grade. It's about seeing your cup as half full and not half empty. Which one is yours?

2 Don't take everything personally and blame yourself.

When your new boy/girlfriend doesn't message you after your recent date, you don't have to automatically assume you did something wrong. There could be many legitimate reasons why they haven't contacted you and if it turns out that they aren't that into you, it's their loss, right? Not everything bad that happens in your life is a result of who you are or what you did. Sometimes, things just don't work out.

3 Stop expecting the worst to happen.

People with negative mindsets catastrophize a lot and believe that whatever can go wrong, will. If your day starts out bad, that doesn't mean it's all going to be downhill from here. The chances are that if you buy into that negative way of thinking, you are setting yourself up for a bad day. Instead, imagine the best outcome and stick with that - it will lift you up instead of making you feel down without a valid reason.

4 You don't have to be perfect.

You don't need to be perfect or excel at whatever you do. It's OK to underperform sometimes and allow space for both success and failure. Setting too high a standard for yourself can often lead to feelings of inadequacy and self-loathing, which isn't good for you. Instead of judging yourself too harshly, cut yourself some slack — we all have off days now and again. You can read more about the power of positive thinking in Chapter 9.

How to stop the downward spiral

Changing the way you see life isn't going to happen overnight, which is why you need to adopt some new habits to help you along the way. These are simple to do and if you practice them often enough, I can promise you that you will start to feel better within yourself.

Learn mindfulness. This is a very effective way to block all of those negative emotions and reactions before they take over. Whenever a thought pops up, pay attention to how it is affecting you. If, for example, you think to yourself, "I'm so overweight," stay with those words. Notice how they are making you feel - unworthy, unattractive, unlovable? Yes, negative self-talk is your worst enemy.

When you observe things like this popping into your mind, give them as little attention as possible. Instead, replace them with empowering thoughts such as, "My body is a part of me and I love it." Try it and see the difference in the way it makes you feel.

Be grateful. Life is beautiful and you should never forget that. Even though it may seem to be full of problems and difficulties now, you can still be grateful for the small things. Before you go to sleep each night, find one thing that you are truly grateful for and give thanks for that. It may be your health, your family, your dog... anything you like. You will feel much more optimistic when you wake up in the morning!

Create an abundance mentality. When you believe that anything is possible if you put your mind to it, you don't get stuck in depressing thoughts of doom and gloom. Let yourself dream, imagine, and aspire for anything you like and focus on making them possible. Follow your dreams and stay true to yourself - this will bring you endless motivation and positivity.

Pursue your passions. If you love playing football, painting, listening to music, dancing, or reading, do it as much as you can. When you spend your time doing whatever fulfills you, the pleasure you receive can plug a lot of gaps in your mental well-being. Do more of what makes you happy and avoid spending time mulling over all of your problems - life is supposed to be fun!

Change your self-talk. This is an easy tactic to talk yourself into feeling better when nothing seems to be going your way. Turn negative sentences into positives like this: avoid using phrases like: *I don't think I can, I'm not sure I am capable, It seems too difficult*.... Instead, begin like this: *I'm sure I can, I'm certain I am capable, I'll give it my best shot.* Believe in your capabilities and make it happen!

Have a laugh. There's no better way to pick yourself up than to laugh and it's a great way to release all of that pent-up negative energy. Watch a comedy or funny TikTok videos and start seeing the brighter side of life. The more you laugh, the less burdened you will feel about your problems. A little humor goes a long way and I highly recommend it!

Take a time-out. Get away from the noise for a while in a quiet spot where you won't be disturbed. Close your eyes for a few minutes and concentrate on your breathing. Let whatever thoughts come into your mind simply drift away. Give yourself a few moments to just exist without the negative energy draining you. Breathe in and let it all out. You'll notice how calm you feel afterward.

If you really want to enjoy your life more, you need to raise your positivity levels and be more optimistic about your future. No matter how hard that seems right now, you can do it if you try. Keep in mind these **six simple rules** and help yourself to make the most of being a teenager today:

- Recognize your triggers. Know what sets them off and avoid them if you can.
- Replace negative habits with healthy, positive ones that improve your wellbeing.

- Remind yourself of what you want in life and think about ways of achieving it.
- Reward yourself to keep motivated and be proud of what you achieve.
- Reach out to someone you trust when you feel overwhelmed and need to talk.
- Relax more and take care of your physical and mental health.

Life can seem complicated and confusing at times, and that's scary. As you struggle to come to terms with the changes going on inside you, remember that it's a natural process and you are strong enough to deal with it. Everything you are experiencing is part of the growing-up process and we've all been through it. As for what's going on around you, you might not be able to change the world, but you can alter how you react to it.

Trust in yourself and remember that life is a gift to be enjoyed, not a prison sentence. Unlock the potential you have inside you to thrive and grow - there's no better time than now!

Helpful tips:

- *The anxiety you feel is real and should be taken seriously.*
- *Changes in the brain can cause a lot of chaos and confusion.*
- *Whatever you are dealing with, positive thinking can help.*
- *Stopping the downward spiral is possible if you really try.*
- *Help yourself by following the six simple rules.*
- *Talk to someone you trust if you need to unload all of that negativity.*

3
GIVE YOURSELF A BREAK - LETTING GO OF SELF-JUDGMENT

"Self-esteem comes from being able to define the world in your own terms and refusing to abide by the judgments of others."
— Oprah Winfrey

How much do you like yourself? A little? A lot? Not at all? That's completely normal at your age because you are trying to figure out who you are.

You are probably comparing yourself to other teens too, and that can be like self-torture as you check out how you measure up against them. I know how that goes, after bringing up two kids of my own.

When my son was 15, he decided that he wanted to stop playing basketball for the local team because he felt self-conscious about being too thin. On top of that, my teenage daughter went through a phase of feeling totally depressed because she didn't look like Taylor Swift!

When you are growing and changing both inside and out, it's hard to accept who you are becoming. Who is this person, you might ask yourself. Do they look as good as Sean or

Maria, are they as smart as Josh or Sam? I bet you think that there are plenty of other people much better looking than you and they are the ones you are comparing yourself to all the time. You probably have quite a few hang-ups about your body, telling yourself things like:

- I'm too fat/thin
- My nose is too big/small
- My hair is too straight/curly
- My chest is too flat
- I'm not pretty/handsome enough
- I'm not tall enough

You could probably add to that list and no doubt, everyone has something going for them except you. I call this the 'ugly duckling' phase, and we've all been through it. I can't think of anyone who hasn't had issues with their appearance when younger, or worried about how they looked. It's completely natural.

The thing is, what can you do about it? When we judge ourselves, we are always a lot more critical than when judging others and it's important to get out of that habit before it goes to extremes.

It's not just our looks we are judgmental about, either. I'm sure you think that you're not as smart as someone else, or as funny. You could be painfully aware of the fact that you don't have any confidence, get tongue-tied when you have to speak in front of others and hate drawing attention to yourself. This awkward phase in your life is full of doubts and you have no confidence in yourself. That's hard to live with, isn't it?

And then, there are those evil thoughts spinning around your head, telling you things like that guy/girl you like doesn't even know you exist, you'll never be picked for the school play as you are useless, and you're never going to get into college. Yes, you are most likely very down on yourself and spend a lot of time stuck in the 'poor me' mode.

Well, as I said earlier, it's all part of the 'ugly duckling' phase but you can make life a little easier if you stop being so self-judgmental. There are enough critics out there who will be more than happy to put you down, so you don't need to do it yourself.

Every time you look in the mirror, you are probably taking a mental note of everything that you think is wrong with you. And you do this on repeat until you believe your imperfections are much more obvious than they really are. Then, you go to your phone and scroll through hundreds of images of perfect pop icons, insanely gorgeous Instagram influencers, and 'friends' having a fantastic lifestyle. That simply confirms your worst suspicions: your life is a bummer.

When you think the same things over and over again, you actually start to believe this augmented reality about yourself. Then, you feel even worse than you did before, so it's a kind of downward spiral. That's why it's important to understand that your negative self-talk is controlling how you feel and you need to do something about that. After all, if you are so hard on yourself, how can you expect anyone else to see you in a positive light?

I know that you desperately want to fit in and might often believe you don't. We all come into this world with that drive to belong to the pack and feeling left-out or different can be a scary thing. It makes us feel isolated, lonely, and unimportant, which is not how anyone should be going through their life. It's a lot more fun to feel connected, popular, accepted, and well-liked, all of which make you more positive, joyful, and happy.

Any insecurities that you have about your looks or abilities stem from a fear of not being accepted and when that happens, your self-confidence can hit rock bottom. Wouldn't you rather feel good about yourself, be reasonably OK with how you looked, and not be too worried about what other kids think of you? If your answer is YES, you need to start silencing that inner critic.

The voice in your head

You know the one, right? The voice that goes on and on about how unattractive or unpopular you are. It never shuts up, driving you insane from morning to night about your big nose, skinny arms, short stature, weird hair... you name it. It's called your 'inner critic' and is very powerful. You might think that it's your best friend because it's telling you the truth but, in fact, it's really your worst enemy.

When you feel unsure about yourself and uncertain of your capabilities and potential, you need someone to tell you that you will be OK. Unfortunately, you tend to be very hard on yourself instead and develop a kind of 'alter ego' or inner voice that constantly criticizes you.

It feeds on your lack of confidence and low self-esteem. The worse you feel about yourself, the louder it gets. It's like your favorite playlist on repeat, reminding you all the time of your flaws and imperfections, and you can't turn it off.

Imagine how different you would feel if you stopped having negative thoughts like:

- I'm ugly
- I'm stupid
- I can't do anything right
- I'm a failure.
- I've got no friends

- I'll never amount to anything

Wouldn't it be great if you could give yourself a break and not have to hear all of this stuff from morning till night? You can, if you follow these simple strategies:

1. **Remove the 'I' word and replace it with 'you'.** Whenever you talk to yourself in your head, you probably make statements like, "I look awful, I don't fit in," and so on. From now on, change the 'I' to 'you', as if you were talking to someone else. This diverts that negative voice and disassociates you from all of its bad talk.
2. **Next, give your inner voice a name** (how about Grinch or Cruella?) When it starts pulling you down, ignore it, just as you would when you hear your folks complaining about your messy room. Your inner voice isn't the authority on who you really are - it's just someone having a go at you and there's no reason why you have to put up with that. Shrug it off with, "There goes the Grinch again..." and stop listening to negative comments.
3. **Never say never.** Instead of saying to yourself, "I never look good in jeans" or "I never feel attractive", remove the word never and start using 'always'. And when the Grinch cuts in with some snide comment like, "You look a mess," reply by saying, "I feel great about myself."
4. **Change the negatives to positives.** It might seem like simple wordplay, but positive thinking can make a massive difference in how you feel. Rather than bringing yourself down, lift yourself up - nobody else is likely to do it for you. Instead of telling yourself you aren't worthy, try saying, "I am capable of doing a lot of things."

5. **Stop focusing on your weaknesses.** No matter what anyone else says (inner Cruella included) don't let them drag you down. Gossip can be nasty and it's the last thing you should be concentrating on now.
6. **Don't imagine the worst outcome.** When faced with a problem, you might automatically go into catastrophe mode, saying things like, "I'll never get a good job," or "I'll never have a boyfriend/girlfriend." Instead of doing that, just concentrate on your feelings and forget about imagined outcomes. You can't predict the future but you can control your present state of happiness.

Why compare yourself to others?

When I was 16, I had to face the reality that I was never going to be a supermodel. At 1.67 meters, my fate was sealed - I didn't have that long, coat-hanger body that was in fashion back then. It was the moment I stopped comparing myself with other girls, as I realized that there was only one Kate Moss, and only one me. Once I started to appreciate my uniqueness, it didn't bother me anymore that I wasn't like anyone else. In fact, I celebrated it!

When you are always comparing yourself to someone else, you'll never feel good. There will always be someone out there who is prettier, smarter, thinner, richer, or more talented than you. It's a loser's game to feel bad about who you are because you can't be anyone else. Sure, you can improve your appearance, widen your social circle, learn new skills, perfect your own talents, but you'll always be you.

At this point in time, you might be struggling to accept your looks or capabilities and it can seem like everyone else is better than you. That's an illusion you've created because you are comparing yourself to people who are different from you.

The way around this is to set your own benchmark – be your own idea of perfection – and stop measuring yourself against other people.

Judge and jury

Why are you so hard on yourself? Is it because you are under pressure to conform, or feel like you aren't as good as everyone else? Whatever the reason, you can be the harshest judge and jury there is. As you go through these teenage years, you are experiencing a lot of new things in your life, from the way your body is growing to expectations put on you to act a certain way. You aren't a kid anymore, but not exactly an adult either, so it can be very confusing.

It's very likely that your self-confidence isn't that high, which makes it easy for you to be vulnerable to criticism. A simple comment by someone else can be hurtful because you internalize it as being true. In the search for your identity, the opinions of others can negatively impact your sense of well-being and take their toll on your self-worth.

Nobody is resistant to criticism, but we don't all believe everything we hear. By the time you reach adulthood, you will have grown a thicker skin and not be as easily affected by negative comments or opinions. Until then, you will probably be more easily influenced by judgments, and turn them into facts.

It's time to stop believing everything you hear, and that includes your own self-judgmental thinking. Judgments are only opinions and they are NOT written in stone. People will say whatever they want, but that doesn't make it true. When someone tells you that you'll never be any good at playing the guitar, why do you believe them? Why not believe in your own talents and skills instead?

You need to start taking a different position and remove self-judgment from your thoughts. Being tough on yourself isn't doing you any good, which is why you have to be more compassionate instead.

Face the facts

The way to do this is by facing the facts and not letting opinions affect the way we feel about ourselves.

Self-judgment increases anxiety, depression, and negative thoughts, while facing the facts helps to put things into a more manageable perspective.

Let's say, for example, that you flunk your chemistry exam. Instead of being judgmental with yourself by saying something like, "I'm so stupid. I can't believe I failed!" replace that statement with, "I feel so frustrated but I'm going to study harder next time." See how that works?

When you remove the judgment, you can still express how you feel but without beating yourself up at the same time. It's not easy to do, but once you get used to looking at facts rather than making negative self-judgments, you'll be able to stay more positive and accepting of who you are. When you start to embrace self-acceptance, you will even feel less anxious and stressed out, which is definitely a bonus.

Accept change

Most of what you are thinking and feeling is normal for someone of your age. As your brain tries to sync with all the hormonal changes going on, it's a bit like updating a computer. Some features are moved around, new software is downloaded, certain apps might be deleted, and others are added that you didn't have before. You might not like the new interface but, unlike your PC, you can't revert to the older version if you're not satisfied with the performance. You just have to get used to it.

You might think that your flaws are bigger than they actually are, and exaggerate aspects of yourself that aren't that obvious to other people. You could also believe that there's something wrong with your personality and ignore other factors in your life that are making you feel unhappy. We all cope differently with problems as they crop up, and at your age, it's part of getting to know yourself better.

- I want you to get into the habit of reminding yourself that many of your so-called shortcomings are not only common but also normal.
- Anyone in your position would feel the same way about their body, their performance at school, their social life, and their inability to cope with pressure.
- It is OK to feel angry, embarrassed, or unable to cope when certain scenarios play out in your life. Nobody would feel good about having too much stress, not feeling physically attractive, or making a bad decision, and that's part of being human.
- Your reactions are usually a result of your brain's desire to solve problems and keep you safe, which is why you often feel nervous, irritated, upset, and frustrated. When you understand that, you can deal with your reactions a lot better.
- Instead of trying to resist change, embrace it and put things into perspective. It's OK to say, "I'm struggling, but I know this is part of growing and learning."

Try some self-compassion

As you are at the age when you experience a lot of stress and feelings of being too self-conscious, your negative inner voice is having a field day. Switching that voice off and tuning in to a kinder, more compassionate inner dialogue will help you to work through your issues. Here's how you can start doing this on a regular basis:

- Whenever you feel upset, angry, or frustrated, take a time out to focus on that particular emotion. Imagine that you are observing it - it doesn't belong to you - it's just something that cropped up in front of you. Take a look at it, without any judgment.
- Allow that feeling to float on by and say something kind to yourself, such as, "I'm a nice person," or "I do my best and that's good enough for me."
- When negativity starts to blur your vision and you feel tempted to come down hard on yourself, think of a positive trait. In your mind, repeat, "I have a wicked sense of humor," or, "I do a lot to help my community." Stay with the good and don't let the bad get to you.
- Be kind to yourself when you make mistakes, just as you would be kind to a good friend of yours when they mess up. You would never scorn them for slipping up, so avoid doing that to yourself. Be your own best friend, not your worst enemy.

Self-compassion doesn't mean lowering your standards or giving up. It's more like a gentle way of nurturing your self-confidence and experiencing positive vibes. When you practice self-compassion, it allows you to face your tough moments without eating away at your self-worth. If you can recognize your failures, then you can learn how to do better next time, because that's what you want, right?

Whenever you notice that you are coming down hard on yourself, place your hand on your heart and say, "I am special.

I am unique. I am me." You will be surprised at the warm glow you feel inside when you do this – it might be the first time that anyone has ever told you these words. You had better believe them!

You are one in a billion

This might sound weird, but you have to remember that 1.2 billion teens in the world are going through exactly the same kind of issues as you right now. When you mess up, tell yourself that you're not the only one who makes mistakes. You certainly aren't the first teen ever in the history of humanity to fail an exam, feel misunderstood, or have an outbreak of acne.

You are one in a billion so connect with that thought and go through these years with more self-love and less self-loathing. You will feel all the better for it.

Helpful tips:

- *Everyone has to go through the ugly duckling phase before turning into a swan.*
- *Your inner critic isn't your friend – it's your worst enemy.*
- *Compare yourself by your own standards, not someone else's.*
- *Judgments are not facts – they are only opinions.*
- *Accept the changes going on inside you and be kind to yourself.*
- *You aren't the only teenager in the world going through this difficult phase.*

4
SELF-ESTEEM & SELF-CONFIDENCE - TEENAGE SUPERPOWERS IN THE MAKING

"Your self-worth is determined by you. You don't have to depend on someone telling you who you are."
— Beyoncé

Everyone talks about the importance of having self-confidence and self-esteem but you may not feel like you have either. What if I told you that self-confidence is something you can learn, and self-esteem can be nurtured?

Not every confident kid you meet is really as sure of themselves as they make out. Even the most popular girl/boy in the class might be faking it. And many introverts have plenty of self-esteem, even if they go unnoticed most of the time. It's a bit confusing but the reason you need to know the difference between self-confidence and self-esteem is so that you can learn to build both.

What's the difference?

When you have confidence in yourself, it means that you have a good grasp of your abilities.

Esteem, on the other hand, is about your sense of self - how you feel about your worthiness and value.

When you have self-esteem, you probably have self-confidence too. If you have low self-esteem, you will find it difficult to be confident about your abilities, although you can always pretend to the outside world that you are fine.

Self-confidence

When you have self-confidence, you know what you are capable of - if you can pass that driving test or do well in that swimming race. You are much more likely to take on new challenges and be aware of your weaknesses. You won't be put off by failure and will work harder next time to achieve your goals, getting more resilient as you do so. Basically, you trust yourself and know what your limitations are.

You don't have to be cocky and loud to prove that you are confident, and a lot of people put on this kind of show even though inside they feel extremely unsure of themselves.

Having self-confidence helps you to face life with a positive state of mind and deal with difficulties more realistically. You are less likely to feel disheartened when things don't go your way and can bounce back more easily from negative outcomes.

By developing self-confidence, you can:

Enjoy life more

Have less self-doubt

Have less anxiety and stress

Be more motivated

Have more energy

Enjoy being with other people

Feel more positive about the future

Self-esteem

When you value yourself, you can say that you have self-esteem. You know your worth and have a high degree of confidence in many areas. Self-esteem allows you to feel good about yourself and be proud of who you are. You don't feel the need to compare yourself to others or be over-critical when things don't go your way. You can handle the storms without feeling battered and torn.

Most people with a high level of self-esteem have been raised in a supportive environment where they felt loved and appreciated. Being put down at an early age doesn't do anything for your sense of worth and can easily make you believe you aren't good enough. But it is possible to turn those preconceptions around. It starts when you begin to believe that you are capable and don't have to be perfect.

By building up your self-esteem, you can:

Feel more able to cope with challenges

Think more highly of yourself

Enjoy better relationships with your peers and adults

Feel happier about your accomplishments

Find it easier to deal with disappointments and failures

Be more likely to achieve your goals

How can you develop more self-confidence?

The first thing you need to realize is that self-confidence comes from within — it's not something you can buy online. The way you interpret external events can have a big impact on you, but it's up to you to find a way to remain positive.

- Believe in yourself

Your opinion matters more than anyone else's, even if you have a lot of different people telling you what's what. You might have relied on the opinion of others up until now to guide you but as you start entering the adult world, you are free to form your own opinions.

Although your parents might have some great ideas, you don't have to compromise all the time to please them. Think about what is best for you instead of relying on others to lead you. When you start to do that, you will gain more confidence in your abilities to be independent.

- Try not to be influenced by others

Instead of following the crowd to fit in, follow your own style of dress, taste in music, or hobbies. I know you might feel the urge to go along with your mates to be liked but honestly, if they are true friends, they will like you no matter how you are. When you stay aligned with your beliefs without feeling that you need validation from someone else, this will allow you to build self-confidence and that's a great feeling.

- Forget about being perfect

If you are always trying to be perfect, you will often be disappointed. It's just not possible to be at your A-game all the time, and no one should expect that. Although it's great to strive for perfection, it's good to accept that you can't always achieve it. Once you let go of that unreasonable demand on yourself, you will feel more content about anything you do achieve. Nobody is perfect and that's just a fact.

- Remove labels

When you are told so many times that you are dumb, slow, or unattractive, it's really easy to start believing that. If you find it difficult to cope with schoolwork and a teacher called you stupid, it doesn't mean that you are. If a boy/girl told you that you were ugly, that doesn't prove they are right. Take a piece of paper and write down all the nasty things you have been called and once you have done that, tear it up into tiny pieces and send it straight to the trash can. You don't need to be labeled by others!

- Create new labels

Make a new list of all the wonderful qualities and abilities you have, such as being honest, kind, great at skateboarding... whatever it is that you feel you are good at - and stick the list on your pc screen or bedroom wall. This is the real you, not what others say about you.

When you start to build self-confidence, you will be much less likely to get hurt or put off by the outside world. You don't need to agree with anyone to fit in or do things that you are uncomfortable with. Instead, you will feel more grounded and able to put your energy into achieving what YOU want, without exceeding your limitations and boundaries.

How can you develop more self-esteem?

Your life might seem like one big problem at the moment, from home to school and back. It's easy to feel down and stressed out when everything gets on top of you but if you can raise your self-esteem, you will begin to enjoy these teenage years a lot more and feel better about yourself. You have to believe that change is possible and although it can take a while, it does happen, so have a little patience and you'll get there eventually.

- Stop thinking negatively

Instead of dwelling on the bad aspects of your life, such as your poor grades or excess weight, focus on your strengths and achievements. You can make a list of five things you are proud of, no matter how insignificant they seem. You could write something like how much you help your parents, take care of a younger sibling, or how well you can dance. Remember this list when you start to feel low and use it to raise your self-esteem.

- Overlook your mistakes

We all make mistakes and that's part of being human. If you are too hard on yourself, it will stop you from moving forward and trying to do better next time. The best way to deal with mistakes is to forgive yourself and stop dwelling on where you went wrong because that negativity will eat away at you. Accept it and think of ways to improve in the future.

- Be adventurous

Who knows what new things you can learn if you give them a try. There's nothing better to help you feel good about yourself than having a go at something new. The satisfaction of pushing your limits will fill you with a sense of pride and that strengthens your belief in your capabilities. Go for it and enjoy the experience!

- Do more for others

When you help somebody else, it can bring you great personal satisfaction, as well as help you to put things into perspective. Volunteer at a local dog shelter or do some charity work and you will soon feel that you are making a difference in the world. That's a great way to raise your self-esteem.

- Be happy with who you are

I mentioned this earlier on, but it's important to remind you that self-acceptance equals happiness. When you feel good about the way you look and your personality, you won't have that overwhelming feeling of dissatisfaction. You can hold your head up high and say, "This is me, and I'm content with that." Of course, if you want to straighten your teeth or dye your hair, go ahead - whatever it takes to make you feel good inside.

- Take care of your body

Not only is sport and exercise good for your physical health, but it also helps to release the 'feel-good' hormones in your brain known as endorphins. As you get used to regular workouts, you will start to notice that you feel less stressed and more optimistic, both of which help you to experience a greater level of self-esteem.

Keep a gratitude journal

To help you raise your self-confidence, it's a really good idea to start keeping a journal. I know you probably hate the idea of writing stuff down as you already have enough notebooks for school. But a journal is different: it's a safe space for you to express yourself and to get more in tune with your emotions.

You can buy some really cool journals online that already have prompts inside to help you navigate through your thoughts. If you don't have one of those and are going to use a normal notebook, here are some examples of what you can write about:

On page one, enter the date. After that, write down:

1. 5 things that made you feel peaceful today
2. 1 example of when you felt proud of yourself
3. 1 thing you enjoyed doing

On the same page, write down:

1. 5 things your friends or family admire about you
2. 1 small success you had today
3. The highlight of your day

After that, write down:

1. Your 3 best attributes
2. 3 unique things about yourself
3. 1 thing you are most proud of

Lastly, write down:

1. 5 things you are thankful for

You can ask yourself the same questions every time you use your journal. It doesn't have to be every day, but the more often you write things down about yourself and your life, the better you will feel. Try to avoid adding negative responses even if you've had a rough day. The point of your journal is to remind you of the good things in life, no matter what problem you are facing.

Express yourself

You might be painfully shy and find it extremely difficult to say what's on your mind or show your feelings. You are worried that people will laugh or make fun of you and can't even open up to your best friend or parents. That can be a lonely place to live and it's a good idea to find ways of expressing yourself without feeling vulnerable.

- **Draw a self-portrait**

Even if you don't think you are good at drawing, take a piece of paper and pencil and sit yourself down in front of the mirror. If you are feeling more ambitious, use a canvas and paints or whatever you can work with and begin to sketch a self-portrait. This will help you to reconnect in a positive light unless you draw something totally abstract and surreal.

Try to keep it realistic and create a true likeness of yourself. It doesn't have to be perfect, as long as you feel it's a decent representation of who you are. Make this a positive experience, noticing all of the features in your face that come together to make up who you are and enjoy feeling good about yourself.

- **Get into music**

Everyone loves music and I'm sure you have your own favorite artists and types of music you like to listen to. Music can have a massive effect on our mood, touching emotions that we don't show to other people a lot of the time.

It can make us relaxed, less stressed, or be a vehicle for our frustration and anger. If you feel that you need to get things out of your system, learning a musical instrument is a good way to channel that because it will allow you to express what you feel in a secure space.

Think about the kind of instrument you would like to try, and arrange a couple of lessons to see how it goes. You might be able to get some tutorials at school or you can watch YouTube videos to learn more. If you do start learning to play the guitar or drums, think of the satisfaction you will feel on accomplishing that - there's nothing better to lift your self-esteem and confidence than acquiring a new skill!

Set yourself regular goals

Another great way to feel good about yourself is to set regular goals that you can work towards. I talked in an earlier chapter about SMART goals, which are specific objectives you can achieve in a certain amount of time that are realistic and measurable. It could be anything from learning to play the saxophone to passing your driving test.

Not only will having goals give you focus, but they will also stop you from feeling negative about yourself. They can give you a reason to get up in the morning and fill you with positive vibes so give it a try. Whatever your goals are, here are a few things to bear in mind:

1. **Start on a positive note**

Begin by saying to yourself, "I can do this," rather than having self-doubts about what you can or can't achieve. This is called a growth mindset, where you set yourself up for success, not failure.

1. **Stay focused on action**

If you want to learn chess by Christmas, think of how often you have to play and arrange your schedule to allow for practice time. Concentrate on each step and don't worry too much about the final outcome - it's the actions that will get you there and the willingness to put in the time.

1. **Make a promise to yourself**

Write down your goal and sign it at the end, just like a contract, making a promise to try to achieve it. Hold yourself accountable for your decisions and see them through. Then celebrate!

1. **Visualize your goal**

Create a mental picture of how you will feel when you reach your target and stay in the moment.

Your brain will believe it's already happened, creating even more motivation for you to move forward. That's because the power of visualization is very strong and when we believe we have already achieved something, it can become a reality.

1. **Get help**

Don't be afraid to ask for help or support if you need to. This will make it easy for you to stay on track instead of giving up because you needed this or that. It's not a sign of weakness to ask for help and can prevent you from losing faith in your abilities.

1. **Reward your efforts**

Every time you reach an important milestone on your way to achieving your goal, treat yourself to a small reward. It could be a candy bar or an evening out - anything that allows you to feel good about getting this far. Keep it up!

1. **Monitor your progress**

Keep checking in with your progress by writing down how far you've come, and what steps you need to take next. Tick off your accomplishments and notice how you are progressing. This is a great motivator to encourage you to keep trying.

1. **Get ready for hiccups**

There could be things in your life that you can't control, which might slow you down or prevent you from reaching your goal. Don't beat yourself up over that and be patient instead. If you are self-sabotaging your efforts, reconsider what you have set out to do - maybe you need to change direction or think of a different, more feasible goal. It's up to you.

1. **Imagine a positive outcome**

There's no point in trying to reach a goal if you are imagining the worst-case scenario. Even if you don't accomplish what you set out to do, that doesn't make you a failure. You can always try again in the future so stay focused on making it work and forget about any catastrophes because that doesn't help.

1. **Remember why you set your goal**

Reminding yourself why you set a specific goal in the first place is important. What motivated you to start working towards it and what does it mean to you to succeed? When you ask these questions, you will remember what made you choose to strive for your target and it will help you to keep going.

Having greater self-confidence and self-esteem will help you to deal with many of the challenges you are facing in these difficult teenage years. Even if you often feel unworthy, incapable, or not good enough, you can develop a more positive outlook over time and be able to handle life with less stress and unhappiness.

Remember to be fair with yourself and listen to your needs, instead of being influenced by other people. Don't apologize for how you feel or the opinions you hold - they are part of who you are.

Stay true to your values and sense of right & wrong, rather than trying to please others or fit in. Enjoy exploring your potential and be proud of yourself, no matter what.

Helpful tips:

- *Self-confidence and self-esteem are two separate things, although they often overlap.*
- *Believe in yourself and your abilities if you want to be happy.*
- *Forget about being perfect or attaching negative labels to yourself.*
- *Accept your flaws and be grateful for what you have.*
- *Keeping a gratitude journal will help you to appreciate your strength and attributes.*
- *Express yourself through art or music and raise your self-esteem.*
- *Set yourself goals and boost your self-confidence when you achieve them.*

THE MOST IMPORTANT DECISIONS YOU'LL EVER MAKE

"If you don't have the information you need to make wise choices, find someone who does."
– Lori Hill

Life is all about making the right decisions, and as a teenager, that can be tricky. You might be torn between making choices that seem attractive to you at the time, and the choices suggested to you by adults that seem boring or not right for you.

Do you drop out of school or stick with it? Do you tell on a friend who is using drugs or keep it to yourself? Do you keep going to church or refuse because you don't believe in that stuff anymore?

Up until now, you probably haven't had to make any serious decisions and usually went along with what everyone else was doing or followed your parent's advice. Now that your thinking has become more progressive, you feel the need to strike out, do your own thing, and assert your individuality.

The problems usually arise when your decisions clash with authority, the society and culture you live in, and within your family unit. I know that you might feel you are fully capable of making your own choices about life but I think it's a good idea to get as much advice as possible before you do anything drastic. The reason for this is that you haven't developed those great decision-making skills yet and won't do so until you have reached adulthood.

Brain networking

A lot of what you do is based on impulses and emotions at the moment because your brain is still trying to get your cognitive (or thinking) powers in order.

In biological terms, different parts of our brain are growing at different rates. This means that the emotional centers at the back are already developing, while your prefrontal cortex, which is responsible for reasoning and decision-making, has a bit of a lag.

Does that make sense?

When you feel overly emotional, confused, frustrated, it's because you are dealing with intense reactions and can't always rely on your rational mind to come in and calm things down. For that reason, any decision you make needs to be weighed up very carefully before you go ahead with it.

Even though you might genuinely believe that you are making the right choices, I've got to tell you that they may not be as sensible as you think they are. That's why you need to hold back, seek counsel, ask a friend, be informed — whatever it takes before you dive in and do something you might regret.

Risks and rewards

We've all taken risks in the past and regretted them, especially in our teen years. I remember jumping off trees that were way too high for me, just to get the approval of my brothers. I also left school way too early because I wanted to start earning money, which I definitely regretted later on. You could say that my reasoning skills were centered on short-term rewards, and not long-term outlooks.

That's part of being young and whatever we experience is a life lesson. Having said that, it doesn't mean we should take dangerous risks or make decisions that can have serious consequences for our future.

When you are at the age of 13-17, the reward center of your brain is very active and whenever you experience fun, winning, or taking a successful risk, you get rewarded with a shot of dopamine.

It's a neurotransmitter that sends you feelings of pleasure and you can feel it whenever you do something that you enjoy. It gives you a kick, which is why it's so easy at this age to get addicted to anything that instantly rewards you, like video games or online gambling. Even likes on your social media feed can trigger dopamine in your brain, giving you a buzz every time you receive a notification or message that you just can't resist checking out.

As you get older, these reward mechanisms are regulated by your prefrontal cortex but, until then, you are wired to seek gratification and new, stimulating experiences. This can get you into trouble by making the wrong decisions and putting yourself at risk.

At the same time, I know you want to test the water and push your boundaries. In that sense, risk-taking is normal for someone your age and it's even an important part of growing up. Knowing where the boundaries are is crucial and there's a big temptation to see how far those boundaries will stretch. I get you.

The problem with this is that you might go too far and don't yet have that safety valve to tell you when you are overdoing things. You have nothing to compare with, other than what you see or hear from friends, and they aren't always good role models to have at this moment. You are intelligent and smart, but can still make the wrong decisions, so it's good to have more awareness of that.

When you search for answers to life's big questions, like "Who am I?" you are in exploration mode and have to learn a lot through trial and error. Most of what you do won't have long-term effects on your future, such as dropping out of the football team. No one can expect you to keep on doing an activity you don't enjoy anymore, even if you have been doing it since you were 6, such as ballet or playing the violin.

None of these decisions are particularly life-changing or risky and are more to do with your brain weeding out the things it isn't interested in anymore. It might upset mom and dad, but they will get over it eventually. New pathways are being created in your brain as you go through adolescence and you have a massive potential to soak up as much new information as you can. You learn easier when the experiences are exciting, which is why you might seek out risky activities on the way.

Common teen problems

Most teens are faced with the same kind of decision-making dilemmas and you can rest assured that you aren't the only one feeling confused about what to do.

Some of the issues will become more prominent as you get older, such as having sex, and not everyone will experience the exact same thing at the same time as you. While you might be more advanced than your friends in some areas, they might be dealing with other problems that you haven't had to face yet.

Here again, it's really important to get advice from a responsible adult, and not rely on friends to tell you what to do.

- **The parent problem**

Most of us have disagreements with our parents when we are teenagers, and we often find it hard to accept their rules when we are determined to do certain things. Wanting to get your nose pierced or have a tattoo, for example, can be a cause of great conflict as you try to assert your will and go against their decisions. You have to remember that your parents want what is best for you, and they might also be having a hard time accepting that you are growing older.

Instead of coming across as stubborn, soften things a bit by asking their advice. See what their real objections are and ask if they will reconsider it in a month, or something like that. The more you go against them, the less chance there is of them agreeing to what you want, so start learning diplomacy if you want to get their go-ahead.

- **School sucks**

You spend a great part of your younger years at school and although you might not like it, it's something that everyone has to go through in life. When you stop taking school seriously or really hate it, you might even be tempted to drop out and not finish your formal education. This could seem like a great idea at the moment, but you need to consider the long-term consequences of this decision.

It's a tough world out there and you need skills and qualifications if you want to find a job and become an independent, responsible adult. You only have a few years at school left to go so should consider that and look at the alternatives.

Leaving school with no qualifications will set you at a disadvantage and might affect your whole future. Talk to your parents, teachers, older relatives, or career officers and look at your options. Maybe you can follow some occupational training or get help with your studies if you are struggling. Don't make rash decisions that you are likely to regret later on.

- **True friends**

How do you choose your friends? Are they mostly schoolmates, neighbors, or kids you met in your sports team or local youth club? More to the point, did you actually choose them, or just hang out with them because you know them and, if that's the case, do you actually like them? I know how important your friends are, but not all of them may be a positive influence in your life. They could be exerting pressure that leads to risky behavior, or you might seek their approval because you have low self-esteem.

Here's the thing: you always have a choice about who your friends are. If you don't actually like someone or don't feel they support you, gradually move away from having as much contact with them. Seek out people you have things in common with, including those who have the same values as you. Make an effort to get to know them better and show that you appreciate their friendship. No one likes to be taken for granted, including you.

- **Dating & Sex**

If you are reaching the stage where you are curious about sex and dating, that's a healthy development and nothing to be ashamed of. What I need to stress here is that sex is a VERY serious subject. You have to do your homework though if you want to avoid unwanted pregnancies, sexually-transmitted diseases, or putting yourself in a vulnerable position.

Dating doesn't have to involve sex and if you feel pressured by a boyfriend/girlfriend to engage in sexual activity, please don't go along with it just to please them.

There is a time and place for everything and although you may want to appear grown-up and mature, sex isn't the way to prove that. It may be very difficult for you to discuss sex with your parents and, here again, your friends aren't normally experts either. Find someone you can confide in if you are thinking of having sex for the first time and learn as much as you can about the implications.

Remember that it's not just about the physical consequences, it also involves your emotional wellbeing. A traumatic experience now can seriously affect your whole mental state and have repercussions in later life. Think very carefully about the whole dating-sex deal and never put yourself in danger. Always let an adult know where you are and be smart about what you do and how far you will go.

- **Addictions**

Depending on who you mix with and where you live, you might be exposed to addictive substances like drugs or alcohol. While a lot of teens use things like cannabis on a recreational basis and enjoy drinking socially, that doesn't mean you have to do it too.

I know you want to fit in and not look like a party pooper, but when you overdo it, get drunk, stoned, or worse, you are adopting a habit that can be very harmful in both the short and long-term.

Do you know the dangers of alcohol abuse, for example? Do you know the effects of drugs on your brain? You might feel the urge to experiment and that's normal, but where are your boundaries? It's vital that you are aware of how addictive certain activities can be, including things like online gaming and excessive social media use.

If you want to be grown up and mature, the best decision you can make is to look after your mind and body - it's a responsibility you owe to yourself.

Who can help you?

Now that you understand all of that, you should have a clearer idea of how some of the decisions you make aren't necessarily the right ones. For that reason, you should get as much guidance and help as possible. That can come from your parents, teachers, social club leaders, mentors, or even reliable information on the internet.

It is vital to get all of the information you need before making decisions that can affect your life and I can't emphasize that strongly enough. You may think you know it all, but you don't - not yet, anyway!

I wouldn't rely on your friends for all of the information you need when it comes to making important decisions because they might not have the answers anyway. Although you may feel that they understand you and have your back, they don't necessarily have the life experience or decision-making capacities that an adult has.

That's why teens can get into trouble, with one often leading the other on, completely unaware of where the boundaries of right and wrong are. Hang out with your friends, by all means, but don't assume that they know more about life than a grown-up — they are probably operating on the same risk-reward mentality as you are at the moment.

Decision-making strategies

If you are thinking of leaving home, having sex for the first time, or dropping out of school, there are some strategies you should follow to make sure you are making the right decision for yourself.

Take your time. Even if you have made your mind up and are determined to go ahead with whatever you've decided, taking some time to weigh up the pros and cons won't hurt. Not all decisions require the same amount of attention but it's still a good idea to share any of your thoughts with someone mature enough to listen and guide you.

Write it down. If you are faced with a problem or dilemma, it's a great idea to write it down so that you can get some clarity about how to resolve it. If, for example, you aren't sure whether to take that weekend job or not, which will leave you less time for studying or relaxing, write down the pros and cons. What will you gain from the weekend job and what will you lose?

Think about what your priorities are – do you want to earn extra money? Is that more important to you at the moment than chilling out or doing homework? When you look at both sides of your decision, you will get a more balanced idea of what to do.

Get the details. Think about what you need to know before you make a decision that could have a long-term effect on your future. Let's say you are thinking of leaving home and you are only 16.

Talk to as many responsible people as you can, asking for their advice and opinions. How much money will you need to live alone? What kind of bills will you be expected to pay? What do you do when you have a burst pipe? How easy is it to manage working and living alone? You may just find that you aren't ready for such a massive change when you get all of the information about how difficult it can be.

What are your priorities? How important is it to you to make the decision like leaving home? Is it worth going it alone and sacrificing all of the home comforts you are used to? Are you prepared to receive criticism from your family or community if you do so? Does your desire for independence come over your need to fit in with any family or cultural values? By asking these questions, you will get a better idea of what is best for you and make a decision based on your best interests.

What options do you have? You'll find that it isn't usually an either/or situation in life. We often have a number of options that we can choose from that are less extreme or risky. If, for example, you are still considering leaving home, think about possible alternatives, such as going to stay with another relative or finding a place to stay at weekends only. It's very rare that you MUST do A or B — there are plenty of other letters in the alphabet to consider.

Think of the consequences. When you want to try something new, consider the consequences of your actions before you go ahead. You should write down the pros and cons of your decision on a piece of paper, this time noting any possible good or bad things that can come out of it. Consider each one and think about how well equipped you are to handle the bad consequences of your decision. Can you deal with them?

What is best for you? At the end of the day, you obviously want to do what's best for you, although you don't always know what that is. By going through the steps above, you should get a good idea of what will work and what won't.

Make a plan. Once you have made your decision, create a plan on how to carry it out. You can be flexible and change it if you come across any obstacles, as long as you stay within those safe boundaries. You can also have a change of heart at any time and aren't forced to go ahead with something just because you told everyone that's what you are going to do. It doesn't matter if you change your mind, you won't lose face or respect.

Rate your decision. Now that you have gone ahead with your decision, how do you feel? Is there anything you would have done differently, or that you regret? Can you change your decision or revert to how things were before? And most importantly, what have you learned from your experience?

Throughout these teen years, you will be tempted to take risks, go against authority, and want to shake up the status quo. All of that is perfectly normal and part of growing up. What you need to consider, though, is which decisions you are making based on sound good sense, and which ones are based on emotional reactions and urges.

There are many temptations out there and if you don't have a lot of self-esteem, you might be pulled into situations that are way over your head. Remember that you are an intelligent, bright person with a mind of your own.

Take the time to consider things before diving in headfirst, and talk your thoughts through with a responsible adult. You can still enjoy being a teen without putting yourself in danger or doing something now that will have a negative effect on your future.

Be smart, talk it through, and don't rush into anything until you are ready. You'll have plenty of opportunities to do whatever you want when the time is right.

Helpful tips:

- *Your brain is rewiring and developing, which explains your inability to always make the right decisions.*
- *It's normal to want to take risks to get instant rewards but not always sensible.*
- *Most teens face the same kind of problems as you are experiencing now.*
- *Reaching out to adults who can help you make the right decisions is crucial.*
- *There are many strategies you can apply to help you make the right decisions.*

6
BODY-SHAMING, DON'T FALL FOR IT

"I'm not going to apologize for who I am and I'm going to actually love the skin that I'm in. I'm not gonna be striving for some other version of myself."
— *Amy Schumer*

I admit it! When I was a teenager, I felt ashamed about the way I looked and often got picked on for being too skinny. At 16, I was still a late developer and my 'boyish' appearance was the subject of many nasty comments by the other girls (and boys) in my class.

I hated having to get changed in the school gym because of that and I wanted so much just to be like all the other girls. When I reached adulthood, I continued to try to hide my physical shape under baggy clothes so that I could avoid being body-shamed by anyone.

I completely get why Billie Eilish, the popular singer, chooses to do the same thing and wears oversized skatewear and track pants. For her, it's all about not being exposed to the type of body shaming that's going on around us all the time. Is she fat, thin, overweight, skinny? Who cares? The artist wants to be recognized for her talent, not for her body, and that's something we should all strive for.

Sometimes, this is hard to do because there are so many stereotypes out there of what is 'perfect', and a lot of people are only too ready to shame you for not looking a certain way. The problem is that, as a teenager, you haven't stopped growing yet but might still feel so self-conscious about how you look. That's why spiteful, nasty comments about your appearance can hurt so much and have a terrible effect on your self-esteem.

Stop body shaming yourself

Most teens go through that phase of not feeling happy with the way they look and it's completely normal. No doubt, you are aware of the changes going on in your body and wish that you could look different.

You might worry about your weight, your height, the size of your biceps, the width of your hips, and everything in between. Criticizing your own appearance because you think it's imperfect is bad enough but when others mock you for it, that's where the term 'body shaming' comes in. Whether it's done in person or online, it can be very damaging and even dangerous.

Media is full of stories of celebrities being either idolized for their flawless bodies or criticized for their imperfections. You yourself are probably a part of that, scrolling through your social media feed and judging someone for putting on weight, losing weight, having cellulite, being too flabby, looking too muscular, being dressed 'inappropriately' for their body type, having or not having cosmetic surgery...The list goes on and on.

It's a pity that society judges other people based on their looks, and even worse when you are doing it to yourself.

Nothing positive can come out of body-shaming and you already have enough issues to deal with at the moment. Worrying about your body is just adding to the problems you face as a teenager.

You can't stop other people from making mean comments about how you look but you can stop being mean to yourself. That's what I'm going to help you with in this chapter so that you can feel good from the outside in, no matter what the shamers say.

Your body is unique

Every time you look in the mirror and make a negative comment about your chest, waist, or butt, you are harming yourself. It's very important to understand that nature has got to run its course and you were born with a particular body type. Whatever size and shape you are, now is the way you are meant to be at this moment in time.

You might lose puppy fat as you reach adulthood, grow broader shoulders, put on extra weight around your hip area, or stay slim. All of these features and changes are normal and the sooner you accept that, the better.

Sure, you can work out, do sports, eat healthily, and take care of your body, but being overly critical about it isn't good for you. Instead of being hard on your appearance, why not focus on the inner qualities you have as a person? You wouldn't expect to have the same personality as someone else, so why try to look the same as them?

Stop that self-criticism

Self-criticism will only make you feel worse about yourself. The negative cycle you might have gotten into can be taking its toll on your physical and mental health and you need to stop that.

If you feel overweight, this could make you develop unhealthy eating habits in an attempt to get thinner. Sometimes, this anxiety about how fat you think you are can lead to serious eating disorders such as bulimia (when you gorge yourself on food before making yourself vomit), anorexia (where you eat hardly anything at all), or a combination of the two.

I understand the pressure you might feel to look like your role models but shaming yourself is not the answer. While it's easy to believe that eating less is the solution, the truth is that your body needs a certain amount of healthy food and nutrients to function and grow. It's way too early for you to start trying to have a 'perfect' body, whatever that means.

Skipping meals or eating less might seem reasonable as you try to get to a size that you think is acceptable, but it could be causing a lot of damage to your body, which can have long-term effects. You might start to suffer from things like malnutrition, loss of muscle mass, and even organ damage. Apart from the physical downside to bad eating habits, you aren't doing your mental health any good.

The constant perception you have of being under or overweight can damage your feelings of self-worth and even cause depression, which is a very serious mental illness. A lot of teenagers fall into this trap and instead of enjoying life, are consumed by dark thoughts about themselves. If you feel that this describes you, please talk to your parents or another responsible adult about it so you can get some guidance and help.

Don't be a bully

You are probably your own worst enemy, bullying yourself about how inadequate you are. If you think your popularity is based on how you look and you don't fit into the current stereotype, you can be a mean critic. With every swipe of your Instagram feed, you are attacking your own worth as you compare yourself to others. Not looking like your favorite influencer, singer, or actor shouldn't make you feel inadequate. If it does, you need to stop using social media as much and start spending more time practicing self-love. You are perfect just the way you are and there's no need to put yourself down because you don't look like someone else.

Stop judging yourself

People will always judge you for things you do or say but when you are always judgmental about your own appearance, you are missing the point. Being a nice person is much more important than what you look like and, hopefully, you will know that we can't judge a book by its cover.

We all make assumptions about people based on their appearance, such as their age, gender, background, wealth, and so on. A lot of the time, these snap-judgments are wrong, and we only gain a better understanding of people when we get to know them. In the same way, you know what you are capable of and your good points, so why keep judging yourself based on how you look? It doesn't make sense if you think about it.

Be your own influencer

You are the most important person in your life at this moment and I don't mean that in a selfish way. What I mean is that you need to look after yourself, mind, body, and soul. As a teenager, anxiety about how you look and the pressures of trying to fit in with your friends, do well at school, and even live up to expectations, can often feel overwhelming. You have enough to worry about without making things a lot harder for yourself.

That's why you need to be the influencer of your own life and follow your truth, not someone else's. Your body is beautiful, no matter what it looks like. Your appearance is unique, and can never be identical to anyone else's. Own it and be proud!

Truth versus fiction

Those cleverly filtered images you see on social media are just that — unreal representations of reality. You know how easy it is to morph your face into something different from what it is using smart apps, right? But there's nothing smart about pretending to be someone you are not, or believing that everyone else you see on social media really looks like that.

You owe it to yourself to accept your face just as it is — freckles, large nose, small eyes, pointed chin, big ears.... Whatever. Beauty is totally relative and not defined by any one person. Instead of getting caught up in that idealistic myth about what beauty is or isn't, accept your own beauty because that's real and authentic!

When I scroll through celebrity social media feeds, everyone is starting to look the same. I can't tell Adele apart from Khloe Kardashian anymore, and there are millions of tutorials on how to look like the model Kylie Jenner or bodybuilder Jeff Seid. That pressure to 'look the same' as everyone else can be self-destructive, especially when a lot of what you see doesn't fit in with your physical appearance or lifestyle.

Stick to your own truth and don't try to be someone you aren't. You will feel much less stressed when you can accept who you are and you stop trying to reach perfection — there is no such thing in real life.

If you have been a victim of body shaming, I'm sure it has left you feeling very hurt and seriously damaged your self-confidence. Those times when you were criticized for your appearance can leave emotional scars that take a while to heal.

I want you to know that loving yourself is the only way to grow into a healthy, happy person and you can start to do that today in three easy steps by **accepting, loving,** and **taking care of your body.**

Accepting Your Body

You could say that there are three general body types we fit into and all of them have weird names. You could be an ectomorph (thin and lean), a mesomorph (naturally muscular), or an endomorph (curvaceous or stocky), which relate to your size and shape.

The size of your bones, the amount of normal body fat and muscle tissue are all programmed into your DNA. As you go through adolescence, these features start to fall into place and you can't change your skeletal structure or fat/muscle distribution. You can increase muscle through weight training or lose weight by dieting as you get older but every physical body has its healthy limitations.

It's important to accept what body type you are because you have to live with it all your life. It's pointless wishing you could be taller, broader, thinner, curvier, or more muscular if you don't have that genetic make-up.

A lot of people go through very painful and often dangerous procedures and surgeries to morph their bodies into a particular way. Although this book isn't about criticizing anyone's decisions, when you start wanting to change who you are, where do you stop?

It's a lot better for your emotional well-being to be happy with what you have. By all means, take care of your appearance and experiment with new hairstyles, clothes, and make-up, but be proud of who you are, no matter what anyone else says.

Loving Your Body

What do you love about your body? If your answer is, 'Not much', think about why that is. What is preventing you from appreciating the way you are? Could it be because you feel different from your friends and role models or is it because someone shamed you into feeling that way?

If it's a case of being criticized for the way you look, it's normal to feel hurt by what others say. Just remember, though, that people say a lot of things but that doesn't make them true. Their opinions are just that — opinions. And, so what if you don't fit the stereotype of what is 'in' at the moment? Focus on what is important to your happiness and not on trying to live up to someone else's standards.

Stop putting your body down in comparison with others and praise it instead. Tell yourself what you like about it and keep repeating that until it becomes a habit. If, for example, you have long legs, a cute butt, or a curvy figure, celebrate that. You are just the way you should be and it's good to remind yourself of that fact every day. Give yourself a high five, no matter what you look like!

Your body isn't just a coat hanger! It's a powerful tool that enables you to do so many things. It makes you a great swimmer, dancer, climber, and runner. It helps you to get around, to carry things, to experience life, and to give hugs. Celebrate its power and continue to be amazed at all it can do for you. Your body is a wonderful creation and one of a kind. Without it, where would you be?

Get in tune with your body and listen to it when it's trying to tell you something. When you are stressed out about exams or feeling exhausted because of your daily schedule, let your body guide you. That might mean taking deeper breaths, eating a decent meal, going for a walk, or lying down for a rest. Your body understands you a lot better than you realize, so listen to it and respect the signals that it's sending you.

Taking Care of Your Body

Your body belongs to you, and it's up to you to nurture it. When you abuse it, you will suffer the consequences. It doesn't ask for much, just a regular supply of food, exercise, and self-care for hygiene and health purposes. Think about what it needs and see to that before you get into a negative thought pattern around your appearance.

Eat healthily so that you have the energy you need to do whatever your day entails. Snacks and sugary drinks might be a nice treat, but it's a lot better for you to eat regular, wholesome meals than to fill up on over-processed, fatty food. Take the time to enjoy your meals and eat slowly instead of making do with fast food alternatives. When you treat your body with respect, it will work better for you and make you feel good about yourself.

Keep moving to enjoy a healthy, strong, fit body. Even if you aren't carrying around excess weight, being skinny doesn't necessarily mean you are fit. You still need to exercise regularly and be physically active. Running, walking, sport, dancing, yoga, whatever is your thing, do it often and have some fun in the process. Sitting at your computer screen or on your cell phone all day isn't good for your body because it needs to be active, and at your age, you've got no excuse.

Being a healthy weight is important but before you go on a crash diet or start consuming high-protein supplements, talk to your parents or health professional about what is the right weight for you. Depending on your age, body type, general health, and lifestyle, you might need to lose or gain weight, but there is a right way to go about this. Even if you want to maintain your current weight, don't go experimenting as if you are an expert — you aren't. Always seek professional advice so you can understand your metabolism and what it needs to keep you healthy.

You don't need a perfect body to have a good body image. When you like your body the way it is, you can boost your feelings about how you look and increase your self-esteem, too. Thankfully, the world of advertising has begun to promote images of men and women who don't fit into the current 'body beautiful' trend.

I've seen some great adverts by big brand names for swimwear, modeled by very beautiful, plus-sized models, and noticed a lot of sports clothing brands getting athletes of all shapes and sizes (including paralympic champions) to advertise their products.

Instead of trying to make those selfies look perfect, show the authentic you and let people know you are happy being yourself. If your social media feed attracts a lot of negative comments that make you feel down on yourself, restrict what you share to your close circle of friends. There's no need to paste your personal images for the whole world to see and you can also unfollow anyone who is promoting toxic ideas about other people.

There are plenty of positive role models out there to suit every body type and you can easily find ones that represent you. Follow those who make you feel good about yourself and say 'no' to anyone who disrespects your appearance.

Rather than letting anyone body shame you, say 'shame on them' for being so small-minded!

Helpful tips:

- *Dress how you want and not to please other people, regardless of your body type.*

- *Body shaming starts with the way you view yourself so avoid negative self-criticism.*
- *You are unique and don't need to compare yourself with celebrities, influencers, or even your friends.*
- *Stop using filters and start believing in your authentic, true self.*
- *Accept your body, love it, and take care of it, your self-esteem will skyrocket.*

7
BULLYING ISN'T COOL - STAND UP TO INTIMIDATION, REPEL GHOSTING AND DEFEAT THE CANCEL CULTURE

"Sitting behind a computer gives people a sense of anonymity, but everyone needs to realize that words - even the ones they write online - have a strong power to hurt people."
—Demi Lovato

Bullying has always been around, it's not something new. In my day, it was usually the big boy picking on the puny one in the school yard. Today, bullying has moved to a whole new level and it can happen to anyone, any time, anywhere.

As a teenager, I'm sure you are aware that a lot of it takes place online, and that's known as cyberbullying.

It's very common for kids to bully each other and can start with first graders in the school playground. By the time you are old enough to have your own smartphone, bullying can happen 24/7, taking over your whole life. It can come in all shapes and forms, from name-calling and body-shaming to spreading rumors and physical violence, none of which are acceptable behaviors.

If you have ever been a victim of bullying or are experiencing it now, you will know how hurtful, humiliating, and often frightening it is. It can make your life a misery and have serious consequences on your emotional and mental health.

If you are bullying someone else, you need to know that it is a form of abuse and is not the right way to behave. It is mean, damaging, and can carry legal penalties if you go too far. Hurting others can never be excused as 'harmless fun', even if it's done with that intention.

Why does bullying happen?

There are a lot of different reasons why bullying happens and some of it has to do with one person trying to control another. You might experience bullying at school or college, where some of your peers are jostling for power, maybe they want to exert some kind of control, or get their kicks out of making fun of others.

They probably have their own emotional problems or hang ups to deal with and enjoy taking that out on someone else. Or, you will find people who attach themselves to a more dominant personality who likes to show off by picking on whoever they think is an easy target.

Anyone can be a victim of bullying and it usually has nothing to do with who you are, although appearance can be a common trigger. If you look different from your schoolmates or stand out for any reason, you can become a victim of bullying, although you could also be singled out for your performance at school. Whether you are a good or a bad student – both are excuses for bullies to target you.

It's a senseless kind of behavior that can go on for a long time when left unchecked. If you are experiencing it right now or know of a friend who is being bullied, you really need to let someone else know about it, otherwise it isn't likely to stop.

What can you do about bullying at school?

You have a number of options if you are being targeted by someone who is maliciously harassing you either verbally or physically at school.

You should report that person to your teachers. The longer you let it go on, the worse it will get, so it's important to make sure you nip it in the bud. It might seem scary to have to report a bully who is threatening you, but your teachers will know how to handle the situation and protect you at the same time.

Gather any evidence you have, like photos of physical wounds they might have caused you and the names of any witnesses you might have. Show them to your teachers or parents and make sure your school keeps a formal record of your complaint. Serious physical assault should always be reported to the police and you can ask your family and school to do this for you.

The more your school knows about the situation, the more measures it can take to help you. Most schools have anti-bullying policies and will do their best to support you until the culprit is stopped. Even if the events take place outside of school, such as when you are walking home, you need to let your teachers know about it.

Although you might get to the point where your life feels so unbearable that you want to change schools, this doesn't always solve the problem. You might go from a familiar environment where you know everyone to a completely unknown one and you are the new face. This could lead to being bullied even more so talk to your parents before you go down this road.

Always tell someone when you feel like you are being bullied, even if it's when you receive nasty comments or are treated badly by someone. Adults are the best people to speak to about this because they will know what steps to take and can intervene in ways you might not be able to.

A lot of your time will be spent on your social media feed and I know that you love connecting with your friends there. Messaging, commenting, and sharing information on your personal online accounts are a way of life for most teens and it would be difficult for you to live without that connection. But, as you probably know, the online space is where a lot of serious bullying occurs and the worst thing about that is it's difficult to get away from it.

Your smartphone or laptop is your lifeline to your besties so you can't just stop using Instagram when someone starts to harass you. You might experience all kinds of harmful behavior online from people you don't even know, including things like insults, mockery, rumor-spreading, harassment, and so on.

Online bullying is so common because people think they can do it without getting caught or have to suffer any consequences. Bullies can also be anonymous, creating fake accounts and usernames, so you might not even know who is really behind it all.

It's a terrible position to be in and can seriously affect how you feel about yourself. Cyberbullying, just like normal bullying, can cause shame, low self-esteem, embarrassment, and fear, as well as do damage to your reputation.

What can you do about online bullying?

Online bullying is difficult to get away from and can be even more harmful than schoolyard bullying because it is constant. Being active on social media and having an online community is probably very important to you so when you become a victim, it can be extremely stressful and seem out of your control.

Teens as young as 13 and 14 use apps like Instagram and Facebook, and recent studies show that almost 60% of teenagers have experienced some kind of cyberbullying on these platforms.

It can take the form of sending, posting, or sharing negative, harmful, false or mean content about you. It might also include sharing personal information that causes you embarrassment or humiliation and crosses the line of what is legal and lawful. You might experience it on social media, in text messages, online chats, forums, message boards, emails, or online gaming communities.

You aren't alone if you find yourself being bullied in any of the above situations. Millions of teens all over the world have gone through or are going through similar experiences. No one should have to put up with it and here are some things you can do to stop it:

1. **Report Cyberbullying to your online provider**

As soon as you feel like you are being harassed or bullied, report the user to your online services provider. No doubt, whoever is doing this to you is violating the terms of service and can get their account blocked or deleted. The big social media companies take bullying very seriously and this can often be a useful step.

1. **Report threats to law enforcement bodies**

If someone is making threats against you, that's a criminal offense and should be reported to the police. They have special units set up to monitor cyberbullying so get your parents to help you report anything that is considered a crime. This includes things like:

- Threats of violence
- Hate speech
- Stalking
- Sending sexually explicit messages or photos
- Taking a photo or video of you in a place where you would expect privacy and putting it on the internet

1. **Don't respond to cyberbullies**

When someone begins to target you, avoid getting involved in conversations with that person or reply in a way that could also be considered bullying. Also, the more airtime you give them, the more you feed into their toxic behavior, so don't engage with them.

1. **Keep a record of any incidents**

Whenever you experience online bullying by internet trolls, keep a record of the person's name and account details. Note down the time and dates of the interactions as well and keep screenshots of any emails or text messages that can be used as evidence. You may need this to prove your case when you report cyberbullying.

1. **Block that bully**

Search your social media websites to find the relevant information on how to block someone from your group or feed. You can also change your settings to control who can or can't contact you, which removes them from having access to you via your account. If you know them personally, talk to them when you next see them and explain exactly why you blocked them.

1. **Unfollow haters**

Instead of giving more power to people who like to make others suffer on social media and are into online shaming, simply unfollow them. You don't need to be a part of that toxic environment and can also encourage other followers and friends to do the same. Rather than being a victim of bullying, speak out against it and reclaim your safe virtual space.

1. **Be careful how you treat others**

It's easy to think that everyone has the same sense of humor as you or that they won't mind being poked fun at. The truth is that we all have our sensitive points and don't like to be called out in public. For that reason, be aware that even if it's not your intention to hurt anyone, sometimes harmless comments can be taken the wrong way. Respect boundaries and take care of how you treat people on social media to avoid being labeled a bully yourself.

You can control who you interact with on your social media feed and there are a lot of tools to help you minimize unwanted comments or messages from bullies so use them to your advantage. No one has the right to chase you off something that connects you to your friends so stand your ground and use smart settings to avoid that happening.

It's not always possible to prevent someone from shaming you and you might find out after the event. It can be totally devastating but remember that today's news is tomorrow's history. A lot of people don't believe everything they see or read on social media anyway so focus on surrounding yourself with those who know you well and will be there to support you until things blow over.

Dealing with Ghosting

While bullies are often 'in your face', some people will just ghost you for no particular reason. Being 'ghosted' means when a person disappears from your life (usually online) without any explanation and it can be very upsetting when it happens. You have no idea why they won't respond to your messages or calls, and they might have even blocked you on social media. It's a cruel thing to experience.

Ghosting is easy enough to do and you might have even ghosted someone yourself, for a number of reasons. Maybe some guy was coming on to you too strongly or a friend let you down and you can't stop being mad at him. While you don't feel like you have to give them any explanation, the person who has been ghosted will be checking their phone constantly, feeling distressed and possibly very hurt.

It's one thing to block someone who has been threatening you, and quite another to end a relationship in that way. You wouldn't like it if it was done to you, so why do it to anyone else?

It might seem like a convenient way out because those awkward face-to-face talks can be difficult, but you can't just go through life ignoring people. Being responsible isn't always easy but how would you feel if someone ghosted you that you cared about?

The way you treat others is a mark of who you are, and it costs nothing to be kind and considerate. If you want to break up with your girl/boyfriend, they are probably going to be upset in any case, but ghosting them is an awful way to go about it.

At least have the decency to meet them, talk to them, explain how you feel, and be accountable for your actions.

Imagine how it would feel if the shoe was on the other foot and someone ghosted you. How would you like it if your new girl/boyfriend dumped you like this or you were frozen out of a group? It's not a great position to be in, especially as you don't know what happened.

Ghosting usually has more to do with the ghoster than the ghostee. You might not have done anything wrong at all and the person ghosting you simply doesn't have the guts to talk to you in person so you should bear that in mind.

If the relationship you had with this person wasn't very serious, it might be futile to keep chasing them after you've tried to contact them once or twice without success. If you were involved in a more serious, long-term relationship, you deserve some explanation. Reach out to them with a message or email and ask them to be honest with you, although don't expect any guarantees that they will get back to you.

No one has the power to make you feel bad about yourself unless you let them. While it's reasonable to feel let down by anyone that has ghosted you, their behavior says more about them than it does you, and you might be better off without them. You can get over it by spending more time hanging out with friends, doing the things you love, and putting yourself first.

You can always be like Casper, the famous friendly ghost, if you want to end a casual relationship kindly online. All you have to do is send a message saying something like, '*It was great getting to know you. I don't feel it's going to work out between us but I wish you all the best for the future. Bye.*' This wouldn't work for long-term, serious relationships but it can be a decent way to end something that you are no longer interested in pursuing. At least you let the other person know where you stand and don't leave them hanging on without any explanation.

Combatting Cancel Culture

In this day and age, everyone has an opinion and plenty of opportunities to share it online with the whole world. No matter what you believe or think, you can spread it all over your social media feed and the internet. The problem is that not everyone will agree with you and you might get some backlash about your views, especially if it is insensitive or hurtful to certain people or groups.

Even public figures like musicians, celebrities, or TV stars have to be careful what they do and say nowadays because anything that can be interpreted as controversial invites the cancel culture to step in. This can take the form of calling someone out for what they said or did, isolating them, taking away support, and removing their status.

You've probably been part of this wave yourself, boycotting and publicly shaming a particular person for an offensive comment they made. It could have been someone from your circle of friends and acquaintances or even a person you have never met before.

Maybe an influencer you follow made an upsetting remark about gender or race and you decide to join the wave of people calling them out on social media. A lot of finger-pointing will usually take place and it can become a free-for-all where users vent their anger and frustration about whoever said what.

What you need to know

Although the cancel culture seems like an empowering way to expose injustice, it can also be very harmful to people who haven't actually done anything wrong. You and your friends might decide to ostracize a classmate who made a homophobic joke. This can be extremely hurtful and upsetting for them, especially if they weren't aware of how sensitive the subject was.

There's a difference between calling someone out for what they say or do and making their life miserable because of it. Canceling anyone is a kind of public punishment that might be way bigger than the 'crime' they committed and if you've ever experienced it yourself, you will know how catastrophic it can be.

Most of the cancel culture plays out on social media, which is where it has gained momentum over recent years. Anyone who is a victim of it can find themselves being unfriended, publicly shamed, blocked, bullied, or threatened. While we are all entitled to our opinions, being judge and jury without considering the damage we are doing to the other person is not cool.

It's a learning process to be called out by your friends or peers when you use offensive words or act inappropriately. Being pulled up by them at the moment you are body-shaming someone lets you know that you are out of order and this is a positive kind of interaction. It's also very important to speak up against racist, sexist, or other unacceptable views when you hear them and you can do this without conflict or bullying.

Canceling someone doesn't teach anyone any lessons. It's more like a punishment that can be very damaging, especially when you are in those sensitive teenage years.

You will know how important your social network is to you and if you get rejected, that can really hurt. It can lead to serious health problems, including depression and suicidal thoughts, as well as leaving you with major trust issues. You might see it as a betrayal by your peers and the after-effects could last well into adulthood.

Being right isn't always the most important thing in life.

You can also express qualities like empathy, compassion, understanding, and even forgiveness. Learn how to discuss your differences with others instead of shutting them down because you think you are in the right. A healthy dialogue is much more useful than trying to bring down anyone who has a different viewpoint to you.

If you are a victim of the cancel culture, take some time to think about why your comments or actions were so hurtful to others. You can try to see it from their point of view and even make an apology if that's possible. If you feel overwhelmed by their reaction to you, it's a good idea to get some support and even talk to a health professional to help you overcome the shame and trauma you are experiencing.

Your teenage years might often feel like walking a tightrope as you try to keep your balance in a world of social media and peer pressure. Sometimes you will be a victim of bullying, ghosting, cancel culture, and other times you might be a perpetrator.

If you want to avoid either, you need to respect yourself and those around you. It's always a good idea to think about how you would like to be treated and approach other people in the same way.

You are going through some testing times, just like all the other teens out there, and it can be hard to navigate everything successfully. It's OK to make mistakes as long as you learn a lesson from them. It's also normal to feel pressured by your friends to do certain things, which is why maintaining your boundaries is vital.

Take care of your physical health by eating correctly, sleeping enough hours, and exercising regularly.

Look after your mental health by talking your problems through with a parent or professional before anxiety and depression set in.

Spend less time online and forget about the internet for a while — it's not going anywhere. Instead, get out of the house more and do what you love, spend real time with friends, and switch off your mobile phone often.

You owe it to yourself!

Helpful tips:

- *Bullying can happen to anyone and being a victim doesn't mean there is something wrong with you.*
- *Don't put up with bullying at school —your teachers can help to stop it.*
- *Learn how to avoid cyberbullying and report it to law enforcement when it becomes serious.*
- *Staying away from toxic situations and people will help you to avoid being a victim.*
- *Be responsible and end relationships face-to-face instead of hurtful ghosting.*
- *Instead of following the cancel culture, think about the harm it can do to the victims.*

8
SOCIAL ANXIETY - SIGNS, SYMPTOMS, AND SOLUTIONS

"It's very isolating. There's a part of my brain that is telling me that you're about to die, you either shut down, freeze or you run. The only thing I can do is go to bed.
—Will Young

I'd like you to meet Sam, a high school student. Sam is constantly worried about embarrassing himself or saying something stupid. He hates having to speak in front of the class and prefers to sit at the back, hoping he won't be noticed. Parties aren't his thing — he would rather die than have to walk into a room full of people — and he feels more comfortable hanging out at home.

His social life is almost non-existent but at least he doesn't have to face any negative judgment from others.

Sam has what we call social anxiety and he's not the only one. Around 7% of the population suffer from **social anxiety disorder** and it's the 3rd most common mental health disorder in the US today.

As a teen, I'm sure that you experience some kind of anxiety when you find yourself in new situations. Social anxiety disorder, often called **social phobia**, is a bit more intense than that. It can affect how you feel every day and make you withdraw from doing all the things you should be enjoying at your age.

Like Sam, you might often feel very self-conscious, distressed, fear being judged, and avoid any social situation where you need to interact. This can prevent you from having friends, boy/girlfriends, and get in the way of normal everyday activities like taking part in sports or social events.

When you feel this way, you might prefer to avoid going out, which then leaves you feeling isolated and lonely. Even though you know that your behavior is probably unreasonable, you still feel trapped in your thoughts and worry about being publicly humiliated or embarrassed. You could even have physical symptoms, such as being nauseous, shaking, sweating, and blushing in normal social situations that others seem to breeze through.

Being asked to stand up in front of the class to answer a question can be a big cringe moment. As you feel yourself going bright red, you can smell your sweaty armpits, your legs begin to wobble, and everyone in the room is glaring at you. It's worse than any scary movie!

Since social anxiety disorder usually becomes more obvious during your teenage years, it can make life very difficult. This is the time when you really seek approval from your peers and feel the need to belong. You need to have good friends and enjoy a great social life so when you are full of social anxiety, it can destroy your chances of either. And it damages your sense of self-esteem, making you feel down and insecure about everything.

Why do I feel this way?

Just like any other phobia, social phobia is a reaction based on fear of something that isn't really dangerous. Your mind might react as if it is, and go into that well-known flight or fight mode. Your adrenaline and cortisol levels spike when this happens, both of which are chemicals associated with stress. These prepare your body for head-on conflict or to look for an escape route.

Although most people handle social situations well, if you have social anxiety your fight or flight mechanism gets triggered too often and in situations where there is no real danger. The fear you experience is real, and your physical reactions back that up, which is why you start to sweat, freeze, and so on. When this happens, you interpret the sensations as truly life-threatening, so prefer to avoid them altogether if you can. While your best friend might think, *'Oh, OK, that's just my heart beating fast because I feel nervous. It's my turn to speak but it's no big deal,'* you will probably say to yourself. *'Uh... my heart is pounding... that's dangerous... I better get out of here....'* See how it works?

It could be that your social phobia started when you were younger and can have something to do with your genetic make-up. We inherit a lot from our parents and one of those things is the way our brain regulates anxiety and stress.

Another reason why you could be experiencing it is due to your temperament — you might be naturally shy, sensitive, and cautious in new situations — which become more pronounced as you reach adolescence. Not everyone who is shy will develop social anxiety but it tends to be more common if you do have that kind of personality.

Social anxiety is often influenced by the way you were brought up, your experiences in life, and the role models you had. If, say, your parents or carers were over-protective, it might have been difficult for you to come into contact with new people or get used to new situations. If your parents were shy, you might have learned that socializing can be stressful and possibly something to avoid. Over time, this could have left you with feelings of anxiety whenever you had to deal with such circumstances.

Throughout your life, you will have experienced a lot of things that go toward shaping who you are today. Any stress you went through in the past could have become a pattern of learned behavior that you have gotten used to. Being pressured to interact when you didn't want to could have made you feel embarrassed or humiliated and you might have picked up phobias from other people. If you were criticized a lot when younger, that can make you have low self-esteem or be scared of making mistakes.

As you can see, there are countless reasons why you might feel anxious in a social setting, all of which are completely understandable.

I want you to know that none of the negative experiences need to dictate how you live your life today or in the future. You can turn things around with some patience, time, and effort.

What are the symptoms of social anxiety?

If you experience social anxiety, you might have thoughts like:

- Being extremely self-critical about who you are and what you look like
- Constantly thinking about the worst-case scenario
- Worrying that you are going to embarrass yourself or say something wrong

- Being terrified about having to speak or perform in public
- Worrying that others will think negatively of you
- Constantly thinking about the worst-case scenario
- You tell yourself things like: *I'm going to mess up, I'm an idiot, They won't like me...'*

It's also possible that you have physical sensations like:

- Stomach pains
- Shaking or trembling
- Blushing
- Sweating
- Feeling short of breath
- Dizziness
- Tense muscles
- Feeling detached from your body

Emotionally, you could feel:

- Anxiety/Worry
- Fear
- Shame
- Sadness
- Helplessness
- Irritability
- Embarrassment

On top of all of the above, you might:

- Skip school
- Steer clear of new activities
- Decline invites to parties
- Stay home at weekends instead of hanging out with

friends
- Refuse to speak or participate in class
- Avoid eating in front of others
- Prefer not to use public washrooms
- Find it hard to be assertive or express your opinions
- Be uncomfortable talking on the phone

All of these feelings and thoughts can take over your life and you might find them difficult to talk about. Everyone else you know seems to be doing just fine and you don't think anyone would understand what you are going through.

If it goes unchecked, social anxiety can lead to intense feelings of loneliness or disappointment over lost opportunities. You missed the school excursions because you just couldn't bring yourself to travel with 50 other people.

You missed out on getting the part in the school play because you were terrified at the thought of having to perform in public. Your school performance can also suffer, with teachers not realizing that your behavior is due to social anxiety.

You might not receive the help and support you need, get picked on for not participating, see your grades drop, and get into trouble because you prefer to skip school.

The truth is that you aren't alone if you suffer from social anxiety but if you want to overcome it, you need to get a grip on it. Many teens receive help from health professionals to overcome it and if you feel you need it, talk to your parents or teachers about getting the right support.

It's not easy to deal with social anxiety but you will find some strategies below to help you to cope. Give yourself some time to manage the anxiety you feel and once you begin to overcome it, you will feel a lot better about yourself and life in general.

1. **You are not alone**

You need to remember this, even though it can often feel as if you are an exception. Millions of people suffer from anxiety of some kind throughout their life in different forms and it can be managed successfully. I still blush when I have to talk in front of a large number of people but I don't pay attention to it anymore when it happens and eventually, I forget about it. Even if other people notice it, I tell myself it's no big deal and, to be honest, it isn't.

1. **Face your fears**

The more you avoid social situations, the bigger your fear of them will become. It's like a giant idea has grown in your mind that all social interactions could be terrifying but, in reality, they aren't.

Your mind is telling you that, and you are now so convinced it is true that you prefer to miss out on all the fun. I understand your fear, but this is a case of looking under the bed and seeing there is no monster there. It takes guts, but you can begin a bit at a time.

Make a list of a few things you would like to do but feel unable to carry out, such as eating in the school canteen or presenting your homework in class.

Pretend to go through the motions at home, practicing sitting at the table, or reading out your essay in front of the mirror. Do that a couple of times until you feel ready to give it a go in real life. When you manage to cross one thing off your list, you will realize that facing your fears actually makes them go away, one step at a time. And, you survived to tell the tale!

1. **Talk yourself out of anxiety**

Say goodbye to that inner critic who is always bringing you down and welcome a new, more positive voice. All the negative self-talk you indulge in isn't helping you. When you say to yourself that you aren't good in social situations, it becomes a 'truth'. How about changing that dialogue and saying something like, '*I get anxious in social situations but I'm going to overcome it?*'

Words have power, and using the right ones will empower you. Rejecting the negative narrative you are replaying in your mind and replacing it with a positive one can help you to approach each situation with a different mindset. Instead of beating yourself up about how you feel, focus on your strong points and achievements.

Stop telling yourself you can't do this or that and, instead, create the possibility that you can. If, for example, you want to go to a party but are worried that you will be too embarrassed to talk to anyone, tell yourself that it's normal to feel like that but you are an interesting person with a lot to say. Concentrate on that thought and don't dwell on what might or might not happen. It's a waste of energy!

1. **Check your breathing**

When you feel stressed, it can affect your breathing which, in turn, can make you even more stressed. That's why you start to feel dizzy, light-headed, and want to vomit. By being aware of your breathing, you can actually control all of those physical symptoms and feel less anxiety.

All you need to do is practice some simple breathing exercises when you start to feel anxiety creeping in, and this will help you to remain calm and more sure of yourself.

You can try breathing exercises any time of the day, no matter where you are.

- Just close your eyes and slowly take a deep breath in.
- Count to 10.
- As you exhale for 10 seconds, visualize all of the tension leaving your body.
- Repeat a couple of times.
- That's it!

There are plenty of short, guided meditations on YouTube that you can do and after a bit of practice, you will notice how much calmer you feel before going into any situation that used to make you feel anxious.

1. **Embrace the discomfort**

I know this might sound kind of weird, but getting used to your discomfort is one way to get over it. Imagine that you have to jump into a swimming pool — you know how to swim, but the thought of the cold water and getting wet is putting you off.

It's a lot easier to make an excuse and disappear before anyone notices you are missing. But what about this: jump in anyway! After the initial shock, you might even enjoy the whole experience. You will soon warm up and be ready to jump back in again and again.

Certain situations can trigger your anxiety but sometimes you have to simply dive in headfirst. It's the thought of what will happen that is holding you back, so you need to push through that and be prepared for a little discomfort. After all, we can't control everything but we can control our thoughts. Once you manage to do that, the sense of achievement will be awesome and you will begin to gain more confidence in your abilities.

1. **Practice makes perfect**

Avoiding situations that make you feel anxious is fine, but the more you do so, the bigger the problem will become. On the opposite side of the coin, the more you expose yourself to those stressful situations, the more used to them you will get. If you can practice one activity that usually fills you with dread, such as making a phone call, the better you will become at it.

Pretend you have to call your math teacher about a homework assignment. Think of what you want to say beforehand (write it down if you want to) then pick up your mobile and imagine they are on the line.

Notice how you feel: Are you breathing correctly? Are your palms getting sweaty? Do you feel light-headed?

Great. Now, repeat the exercise, focusing on what you want to say, but being aware that you might get anxious again. OK, now do it again. Keep on going, checking each time to see what reactions you are experiencing. I bet that by the fifth or sixth time, it will be a lot easier to do and you will have less stress as it feels more like a routine thing.

This kind of practice will also help you to build up a tolerance to your anxiety levels and take away their hold over you.

1. **Accept failure**

There will be times when you think you've got it, only to fail miserably. You didn't manage to stop yourself from wanting to flee and feel your heart pounding in your ears. Not everything will go as you planned but when that happens, just remember that life is like that. The lesson you can learn is that you tried something new — something you thought you just couldn't do a few days or weeks ago. It's OK to fail and move on — you will get another chance to test the waters another time. Hopefully, you will begin to realize that your worst fears are usually not about to come true and it's never the end of the world when things don't work out exactly as you would have liked.

1. **Relax and take it easy!**

You probably don't feel that anxious when you are at home in your safe space. Even so, it's a good idea to get into the habit of learning how to self-soothe. This basically means helping yourself to calm down before your anxiety gets out of control when you are faced with a tense situation. You can practice techniques at home such as breathwork (like the example I mentioned above), do some yoga, learn how to do simple meditation, and enjoy doing exercise.

All of these will give you much greater self-awareness and help you to recognize when anxiety is rising inside you. When you are more tuned in to how you feel, it is possible to control your reactions a lot easier.

What you should avoid doing is drinking too much caffeine, whether that's in coffee or high-energy drinks, eating sugary snacks, and food with a lot of artificial flavorings and colorings. Obviously, I don't need to tell you that taking illegal substances is not the way to deal with your anxiety, no matter what other people say.

1. **Find a support group**

A lot of your anxiety might come from the feeling that no one understands what you are going through, which is why a support group can help. You will discover many teens just like yourself trying to overcome this kind of problem and it's great to know you aren't alone. You will be able to share your concerns with people who know exactly how you feel and get the support that you need.

Just being able to talk about your problem can be such a relief and release a lot of the stress you have been carrying around with you for so long.

1. **What NOT to do**

- Having social anxiety is a serious issue. You should never try to control it or ignore it. The more you see it as something that you need to fight, the more fuel you will give it to grow.
- Don't focus on trying to be perfect. Instead, accept that things can go wrong and try to figure out what steps you can take to overcome them.
- Don't accept social anxiety as a personality trait. While you might have the tendency to be shy or introverted, that doesn't mean you were born with social anxiety. It is a disorder many people have and it is possible to get past it and enjoy a fulfilling life.

Although you might have told your parents or close friends about your anxiety, it's unlikely that you have talked about it to anyone else. If you feel the need to tell someone specific about it, such as a teacher, coach, or new friend, you can always message or email them to say there's something you want to share.

Arrange a quiet place to meet where you can open up about it. Telling someone what you are going through can be very hard, so write a summary down instead if you like. The more you share your problem with others, the easier it will be for them to gain an understanding of your behavior. Not everyone will have heard of social anxiety or know what it means to have it so letting them know how it feels is a positive step to take.

Your social anxiety may disappear as you get older. At the moment, that might seem hard to believe but don't forget that you are going through a very demanding time in your life now as a teenager. There is a lot of pressure on you as you grow and mature, and everyone finds it difficult to cope.

With some support, a lot of self-love, and time, it is possible to get through this difficult period. You may still get nervous or anxious later on in life and feel stressed in certain situations, but you will have learned how to manage your symptoms successfully.

Happiness is just around the corner so keep going!

Helpful tips:

- *Social anxiety disorder, or social phobia is a very common disorder that affects 7% of the population.*
- *There's nothing wrong with your personality when you have social anxiety disorder – it's a mental condition that can be treated.*
- *Anyone can develop social anxiety, depending on their upbringing, genes, and life experience.*
- *The symptoms can affect how you think, feel, and behave in all aspects of your daily life.*
- *Facing your fears, removing negative self-talk, and finding a support group are just some of the ways to deal with the problem.*
- *Help yourself by following a healthy diet, regular exercise, and talking about your anxiety issues.*

9
HELP! I'M A TEENAGER - POWERING UP YOUR POSITIVE

"I wake up every morning believing that today is going to be better than yesterday."
−Will Smith

It's easy for your parents and teachers to say, 'Be positive,' but that's not much use when you've just failed an exam, lost an important soccer game, or your date didn't show up. Life seems to suck most of the time when you are a teenager. It makes more sense to moan about it than to listen to mom or dad — what do they know about your problems, anyway?

True. They might not know exactly how you feel, but they do know that being positive is a much better headspace to be in than thinking everything is doom and gloom. In fact, it's been proven that positivity not only makes you feel more optimistic about your future, but it also keeps you healthier!

We know for sure that there are **multiple health benefits** of positive thinking and optimism, including things like:

- A longer life span

- Less chance of depression
- Less stress
- More resistance to getting ill
- Quicker recovery after an illness
- Better cardio health
- Less risk of death from cancer, respiratory conditions, or infections

None of the above may seem like a big deal to you at the moment because you are young and feel perfectly fit and healthy. The problem is that negativity increases stress, which is linked to ill health in later life and a compromised immune system. Positive thinking helps you to cope with stressful situations, and that's one of the reasons why it's so important, because we all know the damaging effects of long-term stress. It's definitely something you should take seriously now!

Aside from the obvious health benefits of thinking positively, the emotional advantages are enormous. You can go from feeling completely defeated to wonderfully upbeat and able to handle anything that comes your way. That's a great feeling to have because life suddenly becomes better, brighter, and more beautiful.

The downside of negativity

I know you will often feel down, disillusioned, and disappointed when things don't go your way. You fail to get into the university or college you had chosen, your best friend has hooked up with the girl/boy you liked, and you've come out in an acne attack, all in one day.

It's a lot to swallow, especially when you already feel low on self-confidence and your parents keep nagging you about the mess in your room.

Although you might often feel overwhelmed by all the bad stuff going on in your life, getting into a negative cycle isn't going to make you feel any better.

All of those negative thoughts just add to the pain, leaving you feeling hopeless about your future. You have all your life in front of you and it's way too early to paint everything black.

That's why you need to develop a more positive outlook, which is much more than just a catchphrase. It's actually a mindset that you can develop — one that helps you to face the challenges in life with enthusiasm and hope.

I'm sure you don't want to be miserable, and would much rather be enjoying life and having fun. Comparing yourself with others, believing you are a failure, acting impulsively, blaming your problems on other people, suffering from low self-esteem, and feeling hopeless are all negative mindsets to have. Who needs them!

When you start to practice positive thinking, you can overcome these and begin to feel so much better about your life. It just needs a slight shift in perception of what is happening around you and finding the good instead of the bad.

Being positive doesn't mean ignoring the unpleasant things in life; it's more about approaching them in a different way. Rather than expecting the worst-case scenario, being positive helps you to imagine the best possible outcome. It's like seeing the silver lining through the stormy clouds.

If you can manage to do that, life becomes a lot sweeter and you can get through tough times much easier than you imagined. And positivity is also contagious — when you feel good, those positive vibes make you even more attractive, which is always a plus!

How to refocus on the positives

Changing your mindset from minuses to pluses isn't easy. It takes practice and time, but it's totally doable. Think of it as creating a new habit and getting rid of an old one. You have been so used to seeing the bad that you need to retrain your mind to see the good instead. Some of the ways you can start to do this are:

Find what needs to change. What areas of your life do you think negatively about? School, home, friends, your appearance, your abilities? Begin by choosing one in particular, let's say school, and reframing the way you see it. For example, instead of feeling overwhelmed by the amount of homework you have, start seeing it as a positive way for you to learn more and get better grades.

Check your thoughts. Every now and again throughout the day, stop to consider what kind of thoughts are buzzing around your head. Are they mainly negative? Rather than letting them run rampant, replace them with more positive thoughts that make you feel better. For example, if you think you are bad at basketball, change that to, 'The more training I do, the better I'll become.'

Stick with positive people. Don't you feel so much better after hanging out with people who have a positive take on life? That's because you realize that the reason they are so much fun to be around is that they don't moan about life. Their positive energy also rubs off on you, so stick with them and avoid the miserable ones.

Kick that habit of negative self-talk. I've mentioned this before, but you need to hear it again. Pulling yourself down is not the way to feel good. Your inner critic has far too much power over you and you have to replace it with a kinder, more compassionate voice. When a negative thought comes into your mind, talk over it with words of empowerment. You are a wonderful person and grateful for all you have in life. Make that your mantra!

Filter out the bad. Life isn't always a walk in the park - bad things happen and that's just how it is. But you can see the good when you filter out what you don't need. Having a great day with friends then going home to dwell on the fact that you are overweight (in your eyes) is a no-no. Stay away from those negative thoughts and focus on the fun time you had earlier on.

Stop blaming yourself. Not everything that goes wrong is a reflection of you as a person. Instead of personalizing bad outcomes with statements like, 'Why me?', get over that victim mentality by saying, 'Hey, it doesn't always work out the way I wanted.'

Avoid the blame game. When you are tempted to blame someone else for the way you feel, think again. Only you can control what you think and feel, no one else. If your parents are bugging you for getting low grades, don't blame them for being concerned or upset. Take ownership of your actions and work on getting better grades. It's you that benefits, after all.

Get rid of the magnifying glass. A tiny problem can become a huge failure in your eyes if you focus on it too much. This can leave you feeling overwhelmed and lacking control of the situation. When your friend is short-tempered with you, don't pay too much attention. They might be having a bad day or going through stuff you don't know about so just leave it. Avoid making a big deal out of it, starting an argument, and letting the situation snowball.

Start seeing the color 'gray'. Not everything is black and white in life — there is a lot of gray in between. When it comes to making choices and decisions, there are always alternatives and other possibilities to explore. If you can be flexible, you will feel much more positive about what you CAN do and less worried about what you CAN'T.

Stop aiming for perfection. A lot of disappointment comes when you set the bar too high and have impossible expectations. When you know what your strengths and weaknesses are, you will have a more balanced view of what is and isn't possible and that's a good thing. Negativity sneaks in when you set yourself up for failure, believing something will happen that just isn't realistic, so stay grounded and accept reality.

At your age, it's difficult to look too far ahead into the future and imagine where you will be in one, five, or ten years' time. That's why it's so important to focus on your present and make the most of your life now. One way to do this is by turning your attention to micro-moments — those everyday habits and attitudes that make you feel happy and support your mental health.

Want to feel good?

You know how happy you feel when you have some good news or enjoy a great time with friends and family? You can use those positive emotions of joy, love, and contentment as building blocks of how you want to feel all the time and not just now and again. The way to do this is by creating a kind of positive feedback loop that helps your brain to rewire. It's not as difficult as it sounds and you don't need to be a neuroscientist!

When you feel happy, you want to hold onto that emotion and one way to achieve that is by repeatedly doing the things you love. Instead of spending your spare time sitting in your bedroom, get involved in activities that you enjoy.

- If you like a particular sport, arrange weekly games with friends.
- If you are into art, check out any exhibitions in your local galleries.
- If you enjoy home crafts, put aside a set time each week for your creative talents.
- If you love animals, volunteer to help at your local shelter.
- Get involved with the community and help in fundraisers or charity events.
- If you don't know what you like doing, sign up for a new sport, join a club, check out after-school activities.
- Try out new hobbies with friends and if you don't enjoy them, look for something else.

Explore the possibilities that new experiences bring. The thrill you get from discovering something new will fill you with greater enthusiasm and zest for life. You will soon forget any other problems you were dwelling on while sitting alone in your bedroom.

You can make new friends, meet people with different interests to you, and create even stronger bonds. All of this helps you to feel better about yourself and enjoy more positive emotions.

As time goes by, you will get used to being happier, with each positive experience reinforcing your outlook on life. This is where personal growth and well-being start to form deep roots that will help you to overcome all of the negativity you feel.

Find your inner strengths

Pushing past the fear is difficult to do when you are in your teens because there are a lot of unknowns out there. But if you never try, how will you know what you are capable of?

I'm not talking about taking dangerous risks here or doing anything that is outside of your comfort zone. What I mean is seeing where your natural strengths and weaknesses lie. Knowing what you are good at helps you to build self-esteem and will give you a great sense of accomplishment. Anything that puts you to the test, be it to do with your physical or intellectual abilities, can be an eye-opener, revealing talents you might not have known you had.

We all have inner strengths but sometimes these go untapped because we don't stretch ourselves enough. You might not have any idea what your strong points are so here's a list of things for you to think about.

- CreativityEmpathy
- FairnessLeadership
- TeamworkPatience
- ModestySelf-discipline
- GratitudeHumor
- CuriosityOpen-mindedness
- Love of LearningPerspective
- HonestyBravery
- PersistenceKindness

Often, it's only when we put ourselves out there that we realize our superpowers. You might not know how brave you are until you try rock climbing, or how creative you are until you start writing. Give it a shot and see what happens!

Happiness comes when we do things we enjoy and feel good about our abilities. By discovering your strengths, it will be easier to direct your energy into anything that brings fulfillment and positivity. Each day can bring you new surprises and teach you to work through problems with greater confidence and optimism. That's a good headspace to be in!

Making positive thinking a habit

Feeling good takes practice and won't happen overnight, especially if you have been used to feeling down and hopeless. You can help yourself to feel more positive by using the following strategies:

- **Recognize** the triggers that kick you into a bad headspace and work out how to avoid them. Arguing with your parents, for example, is sure to grind you down, so how about making sure you are doing your part to preempt any complaints they might have about your behavior?
- **Replace** a bad habit with a good one. If you spend most of your free time on your pc, for example, arrange to go for a run or a walk instead once a day. This means less screen time and more fresh air — what could be better!
- **Remember** to make a list of all the things you are thankful for in life and be grateful for them every day. Gratitude is an empowering feeling and helps you to feel happier, no matter what your situation is.
- **Reward** yourself every time you reach a personal goal or milestone. It doesn't have to be something big or expensive. You could, for instance, treat yourself to a night out with friends or a trip to the cinema.
- **Recall** your strengths and think about new hobbies or activities that will enable you to practice them. Good with kids? Look for a weekend babysitting job. Enjoy teamwork? Create a study group with fellow students. Whatever it is you are good at, do more of it!

Set your goals

One way of feeling more positive about life is to set goals that you can work towards. You get a sense of direction when you have something to look forward to in the future and it's a lot easier to stay motivated and positive. Nothing can beat that feeling of elation when you achieve it, too!

If you find it difficult to think of what kind of short-term goals to have, try the **WOOP** goal-setting tool. This is a free app you can download to your smartphone and it's a great way to develop small goals (less than 30 days timeline).

Let's say that you decide to organize an after-school chess club and see how to make that happen.

W stands for what you **wish** for. It has to be something feasible and might need at least 20 students to join.

O is for **outcome**. What would you like to see come out of fulfilling your wish? Maybe you get the chance to play more chess, hone your skills, introduce others to the game, or expand your social life.

O relates to the main inner **obstacle** that stands in the way of you fulfilling your wish. Maybe not enough people are interested or can't attend on the designated days.

P is for your **plan**. What action can you take to overcome your obstacle? Put flyers up at school and hand leaflets out to other students? Have a choice of days when they can come to the activity?

The app guides you through setting WOOP goals (you can also do this on their website), and it lets you track your progress as well. You can set short or longer timeframes, depending on your goals, but remember that the shorter timeframes prompt you to take action right away, while longer ones might need more dedication.

If you want to establish some long-term goals, you can follow the **SMART** technique that I mentioned in Chapter 2. This means that each goal you set should be:

Specific: Something like getting into a particular university or finding a summer job.

Measurable: You should be able to measure your progress as you move toward your goal.

Achievable: It's no good setting a goal that is really only a pipedream, like becoming an astronaut if you hate math or physics.

Realistic: Can you actually save up enough money to go on vacation this summer with friends or is it unrealistic?

Time-related: Do you have enough time to realize your goal or are you cutting it too close?

Keep a positive emotion journal

It's a great idea to keep a journal of all the times you felt good about your life. This is different from a gratitude journal because it's a place for you to note down the times when you felt great. Optimism grows when you experience or evoke positive emotions like joy and inspiration, which also make you feel more self-confident.

All you need to do is find a notebook and jot down the answers to the questions below. For each prompt, try to recall positive feelings based on good times, memories, images, and even songs that pop into your mind.

Hope

When did you feel optimism and hope?

When did you go through a tough time but believed it would turn out well?

When did you solve a problem that made your life easier?

Awe

When did you feel in awe of your surroundings?

When were you bowled over by something beautiful?

When did you feel that you were part of something much bigger?

Joy

When did you feel absolute joy?

When did everything seem just perfect?

When did you feel totally content?

Gratitude

When did you feel grateful for someone or something?

What is the one thing you treasure most in life?

When do you feel like giving back for what you have received?

Inspiration

When do you feel the most inspired?

What did you achieve?

Keep the journal by your bed and update it often. You can go back to it every time you feel let down, hopeless, and filled with negative thoughts. Add any other positive emotions that you experience to your journal as time goes by.

Life is what we make it and, although there will be tough moments, you have the ability to see everything in a more positive light. Think of any difficulty you have faced in the past and consider what you learned from it. Look at your present and pick out 3 good things that contribute to your happiness. Imagine what future you would like for yourself and notice the increased positive emotions you feel when thinking about that.

Train your brain to be optimistic and stop focusing on all the negatives. Surround yourself with positive people and enjoy experiencing the power of positivity every day!

Helpful tips:

- *More positivity leads to less stress and better health.*
- *When you focus on the positives, life becomes exciting and enjoyable.*
- *Changing your mindset, being with positive people, and getting rid of negative self-talk bring a lot of benefits.*
- *Removing self-blame and filtering out the bad keeps you upbeat and positive.*
- *Finding your inner strengths will fill you with renewed self-confidence.*
- *Negativity is a bad habit that you can unlearn.*
- *WOOP and SMART goals bring you motivation and a sense of achievement.*
- *A positivity journal will remind you of all the good in your life.*

CONCLUSION

"It helps to even look in the mirror—and it sounds so cheesy—but if you just look in the mirror and say, 'You are beautiful,' and 'You are worthy,' those things really help you."
—Demi Lovato

Many of the most popular teen idols today have gone through similar tough times to you when they were of a similar age. It's not easy for anyone to face the ups and downs of adolescence without struggling with issues like little self-worth and low self-esteem. You are not alone if that's how you feel but I hope this book has given you a lot of ideas on how to get through the storm.

Having self-love doesn't mean being selfish or only thinking of yourself. It's more to do with feeling good ABOUT yourself and making your happiness a priority. You don't need a lot of money to do it or come from a privileged background. It has nothing to do with where you live, what you look like, or your family life. It has EVERYTHING to do with how well you treat yourself.

Self-love is exactly what it says: loving the person you are, warts and all. Even though you might not feel good enough, pretty enough, or smart enough, believe me when I say you are all those things, and then some!

But you need to believe that for yourself and it begins with valuing your own worth, celebrating your uniqueness, and embracing positive thinking in your life. I'm sure you can do that if you give it a shot.

When you practice self-love, you are honoring your right to happiness. You deserve that and should be able to enjoy it, especially now that you are growing and maturing. An exciting life awaits you and you can begin to make the most of it at this very moment. When you feel confident, positive, and full of joy, everything just keeps getting better and better so why wait?

Remember that self-love comes from within and you are responsible for your thoughts and feelings. Despite all of the outside pressures to fit in and look or behave a certain way, it's up to you to create the life you want.

When you love yourself deeply, you will be filled with an amazing energy that can help you to achieve your dreams!

In this book, I've gone through some of the key elements you need to focus on to achieve that and I hope you will start using them in your life.

We looked at why you matter and how to make yourself the star of your story. We also learned how to stop the anxiety you feel as you try to navigate the mood swings that come with adolescence. I hope you gained a lot from that. Self-judgment was another topic we delved into, with tips on how to prevent it from taking control over you, as well as how to build self-esteem and confidence.

At your age, you will often find yourself facing dilemmas, and we walked through the most effective ways to make the right decisions that serve your best interests. We looked at the pressures you might feel to look a certain way, how to deal with body-shaming, and why you don't need to compare yourself to other people. I'm sure you found the chapter on bullying helpful too, and picked up some useful tips on how to handle that in real life and online, as well as ways to cope with ghosting and the cancel culture.

We also covered social anxiety, which affects a lot of teens, with plenty of guidance on how to overcome your fears and phobias. And, of course, we talked about the benefits of positive thinking and how it can change your whole outlook on life.

I just want to remind you that you are a unique individual with the potential to be your own influencer. You don't have to feel that something is wrong with you because you don't fit the stereotype. Through self-love, you will discover just how special you really are.

Remember to:

1. **Accept yourself for who you are**
2. **Prioritize your needs**
3. **Maintain your boundaries**
4. **Use positive self-talk**
5. **Embrace your individuality**
6. **Stop trying to be perfect**
7. **Take care of your body**
8. **Make time for self-care**
9. **Focus on your inner strengths**
10. **Practice gratitude every day**

Last but not least, learn to love yourself deeply and glow with confidence because you deserve it!

Rebecca

P.S

Make An Author Happy Today!

I hope you found this book helpful. If you did, I would be eternally grateful if you could spend a couple of minutes writing a review on Amazon.

When you post a review, it makes a huge difference in helping more readers find my book.

Your review would make my day

Thanking you in advance

Rebecca

Other books by Rebecca Collins

Positive Life Skills For Teens

Love Yourself Deeply

How To Make Friends Easily

The Art Of Manifesting Money

Love Yourself Deeply/How To Make Friends Easily 2 in 1 Book

A FREE GIFT FROM REBECCA

10 Weekly Issues of Rebecca's life-changing newsletter "Reclaim Your Power" Rebecca covers Self Love, Self Esteem, Making Friends, increasing your confidence and getting your life back, & Living a Life of Freedom.

https://rebecca.subscribemenow.com/

Scan Me Now!

www.ingramcontent.com/pod-product-compliance
Lightning Source LLC
Chambersburg PA
CBHW051701160426
43209CB00004B/987